NATURE'S
CHILDREN

The frontispiece is a photograph of the
author's two children.

NATURE'S CHILDREN

A GUIDE TO ORGANIC FOODS AND HERBAL REMEDIES FOR CHILDREN

Juliette de Baïracli Levy

Foreword by Helen and Scott Nearing

*With Twenty Herb Drawings
by Heather Wood*

SCHOCKEN BOOKS · NEW YORK

CONTENTS

*Scattered throughout the text are twenty
herb drawings by Heather Wood.*

I arm for your sake,
Cast off slough, despondency, fear,
Wearing you on my breast
As Rupert's knights wore lace over armour.
        —*Anna Zaruweska,*
            "The Children"

FOREWORD

We met Juliette, our gypsy friend, in a casual encounter twenty-four years ago in Tecate, Mexico. She was squatting on the ground in front of her adobe cabin when we came across her tending her tiny organic garden. She shone with warm friendliness as we began chatting, and we found many things in common: organic gardening, vegetarianism, fasting, love of the wilderness, of animals and nature. We spent large parts of the next few weeks tramping the dry, rolling Mexican hills with her, exchanging ideas and especially absorbing her extraordinary knowledge of herbs and healing.

She was an original "nature girl," wild and free, completely unattached, except to her love of life, animals, nature, and a few of the right kind of people.

Through the ensuing years she and we wandered over much of the earth, rarely meeting but always keeping in some kind of touch. We sent her our books as they were written and published. She sent us her books on gypsy life and, notably, her *Look! The Wild Swans*, a fanciful and poignant novel peopled with weird characters and full of the fascinating lore of healing by natural methods and of organic living.

Years passed and our next extended contact with her was in Israel, where she perched like a bird in "Jaouna," a tiny cottage in Rosh Pinna, northern Galilee, near the Golan Heights border. There she was living precariously with her daughter and her dogs, writing about her falcon and owl friends and picking herbs on the nearby hills for a living. Most of the dwellings near her had been leveled during the Six-Day War. Her house was spared because, as she described it, "the pine trees in front of my place caught the Syrian shells in their arms and exploded them.

The pine branches were badly torn, but the trees have mostly survived."

She has brought up her children to be sturdy specimens of her way of life. She has much out-of-the-way wisdom to impart to the young hippies of today. She lives a life as devoid of artifacts and pretence as one can live in the modern world. She bathes in the cold waters of Lake Galilee. She lives mainly on fruit and nuts. She will always be a gypsy, living close to nature, as far from civilization as she can get.

This is typical Juliette: "At the heart of all, for Nature children, there will always remain a core of love for natural life, for the fresh vegetables and fruits and whole-grains, for the sun and the rain, the moon and the wind, and for snow—and for beautiful things in general, because their bodies and minds were formed out of such things when in their mother's womb and in their infancy and childhood."

Here in this book is inestimably good advice on natural living —for young mothers and fathers, for grandparents, and for all those who want health and sanity in youth, middle age, and declining years. As a Dr. William Vaughn put it in *The New-landers Cure* (London, 1630):

> Yee, that bee Parents, shall heere learne to weane your Infants with a better Dyet than with Flesh and Fish; which will rot and corrupt their tender bodies.
>
> Yee, that be Rich, accept this Treasure, Divine Sobriety, which will infuse into your hearts modest contentment.
>
> Yee, that be Poore, shall heere learne Frugality, at a cheepe rate.
>
> Yee, that be Young, shall be taught continency.
>
> Yee, that are Elder, and therefore should be wiser, shall meete here with health and long life.

HELEN and SCOTT NEARING

Spring 1971

BASIL (*Ocimum basilicum*)

CHAMOMILE (*Athemis cotula*)

COMFREY (*Symphytum officinale*)

DANDELION (*Taraxacum officinale*)

I

THE MOTHER

The health of every family begins with the mother. She is the tree from which the healthy fruit must come. All primitive peoples recognize this, and there are numerous simple laws which the mother is taught to follow to ensure easy and almost painless childbirth and the production of healthy stalwart infants who sleep well and vigorously drink their mother's milk.

From the first moment that conception is known, the mother should plan a daily régime for building the mental and bodily health of the child who for nine months will be growing within her and sharing her thoughts and food for better or worse.

A happy mind, and gladness in the fulfilment of motherhood, are the first requirements for mental health in both mother and the forming child. A vast number of people, especially in modern times, are barren, lonely. Pregnancy should be a daily song of triumph and thanksgiving in a woman's mind and heart. It is good to be in true kinship with Nature, with the budding fruit trees and the wild flowers and herbs, and to understand the meaning of the songs of the nesting birds (and why the swifts scream as they travel the high skies) and to share the contentment of the animals in the pastures awaiting the coming of their young ones.

Of all the basic rules for healthy birth, the first one must be the necessity of daily physical exercise. In the Western world it seems that pregnancy is the one time when women choose to take less exercise than usual—and really the modern woman takes scarcely any hard exercise at all in her daily life. 'Toil hard, walk far', say the Gypsies and Bedouin Arab women as their recipe for ensuring healthy pregnancies and good condition of their bodies. And most of them manage their child-births at home without the need of clinics or hospitals. I have lived among them and can say that they do what they recommend, and work hard in the fields and around their firesides almost to the hour of birth: and their mares and she-camels also are ridden to the time of birth.

During the prenatal months a woman's body must be kept slim and hard in order to prevent formation of a big burdensome child.which will, from its unnatural size, make for difficult childbirth and ruin beyond recovery the figure of the mother.

Another healthy rule is the daily bath. All creatures seek water (even owls! I was surprised to see how well my pet owls like their bath), and there is a reason for this. Water keeps the skin tissues in good tone and relieves nervous tension, as well, of course, as ensuring the elementary fact of simple cleanliness.

Gypsies like to pull in their waggons close to running water. Apart from the practical benefits of being close to water, it is considered good for their pregnant women, for their peace of mind and gladness of heart. There is nearly always a pregnant woman in a Gypsy family, for the Children of Nature follow the ways of Nature, and every two years a new baby is born to the majority of the mature women—one year allotted to create a child, and one year for the provision of abundant and healthful breast milk. As Gypsy men often have two wives, there is then a new baby in the family every year.

Mahomet is said to have given the Gypsies fertility above that of all other peoples. For it is said that Gypsies saved the Prophet's life when he was dying from an unknown poison. They brought him a strange herb, today called rue, which is known to surpass all plants as an antidote for poisons of all kinds: and Mahomet promised the Gypsies many children.

Air and (limited) sunbathing of the entire body are also powerful health aids in pregnancy. Sunbathing should follow, not precede, water bathing, for water will remove the vitamins deposited in skin tissue following a sun bath. The early and late hours of the day are the most beneficial for sunbathing. The feet should face North, if possible, and head and feet should always be covered. If work is not being done and rest is managed during the sun bath, then cool green leaves can be placed over the eyes, or strips of cucumber peel: all very soothing.

Vegetable oil applied lightly to the body helps to increase the benefits from the sun, and in pregnancy it aids suppleness of breasts and abdominal area.

Oil should not be applied undiluted to the skin, but rubbed on from a large swab of cotton wool previously dampened in plain water; or water with a few drops of vinegar added is better, and buttermilk is excellent instead of water.

Why use monotonous plain oils, when a short spell of work can turn such oils into aromatic lotions? It is easy to collect fragrant flowers and leaves, pound them into a pulp and add them to the oils and infuse them in glass bottles or jars, well-stoppered, in sunlight or in a warm oven. When hot sun is available, it is preferable to stand the bottles in a container of sand. This attracts and holds the sun-heat. Use about two tablespoons of flowers, and/or leaves, to every pint of oil, add also a dessertspoon of vinegar per pint of oil to help break up the plant matter. Herbs which I use most are sprigs of garden lavender, rosemary, southernwood and wild meadowsweet, woodruff, elder-blossom, briar-rose, gorse. Such give healing powers to the oils as well as sweet odours.

Cold bathing is natural and advisable. Hot bathing is unnatural and enervating. But a weekly hot bath is needed for cleansing the skin, as so many people have to endure a grimy environment in this modern world. Bath water too can be improved by aromatic substances, such as drops of pine resin and natural flower extracts, or the crude plant material such as pine needles, eucalyptus leaves, slivers of cinnamon wood, the flat compound blossom heads of elder blossom, all infused by placing first in a square of butter-muslin; place the tied-up square into the hot water while the bath is running and keep this in the water during bathing.

As for exercise: half of the ills of modern mankind are caused by lack of this. All members of the animal kingdom bend, leap, run if they have limbs. Only man seems content to stay stationary with rigid limbs.

In pregnancy natural exercise is always best, such as fast walking, running, swimming, horse-riding, hill-climbing. If this cannot be managed during the week, it can be confined to weekends. When natural exercise is impossible, then the simple bending exercises which are taught in school can be used. One can practise dry swimming, lying on a rug on the floor. It was noted in World War II that women porters, getting much exercise in their railway work, and lifting heavy weights, had very easy pregnancies.

Lack of exercise in pregnancy means slack muscles, excess of fluid around the child, swollen limbs and often varicose veins. I always felt a great need for hard exercise, such as tree-felling and axeing and sawing, as well as daily swimming, in winter as well as summer, and in both my pregnancies my children were so small that people never saw that I was going to have a child, and when I carried my new-born baby in my arms they wondered from where I had obtained him, and later—her!

All my life I have kept dogs, and the greyhound breeds are my favourites: they possess the speed of the wind in their feet. The females are running and hunting up to the day when they whelp their litters. Through the nine weeks of pregnancy their bodies keep so slim and lithe that it is often most difficult to tell if they are in whelp or not, and this remains a mystery until the very hour of birth. The greyhound breeds are known for the ease with which they produce their young.

Sleep must come after exercise, and again exercise must follow sleep. It is well proved that the best hours of sleep are the natural ones, which means from dusk to dawn. The hours between dusk and midnight really are worth twice as much as the hours from midnight to dawn.

Monks and nuns who take a scientific interest in sleep, since they want to be awake during the hours of greatest mental alertness, usually sleep at dusk and awake around three in the morning. Too many of the human race, under-exercised and over-fed, seem to exist in a stupor of sleep taken at the wrong hours.

The question of what and how to eat during pregnancy is immensely important, as we all accept the dogma that we are what we eat. Daily the food intake builds up the body or destroys the body, all is dependent on whether natural vital foods are eaten, or unnatural devitalized ones. By the time they are

16

ready for pregnancy, most women should have found out what is good for them to eat, and do not need such instruction either from books or from individuals. Therefore I shall only give a few basic rules which I was pleased to learn from such a great medical writer as Professor Edmund Bordeux Szekely, whom I knew personally, and from Dr. Douglas Latto, the gynaecologist whose personal advice greatly helped me, and lastly the so-called 'simple people', the Gypsies, wandering Bedouins, and others who have no need of doctors in childbirth: as I, too, had no need.

The simple rule to use when choosing foods, is to take only natural things. Cereals, with the exception of sweet-corn and barley and wheat, have to be prepared before they can be digested by man. Corn, cut fresh, can be eaten raw, and barley needs only to be soaked in a shallow covering of water from twenty-four to forty-eight hours to be palatable and digestible. Sprouted wheat can be eaten raw. All other vegetarian or dairy foods can be eaten natural and raw, direct from wild country-side, garden, orchard and dairy—or from the greengrocer's shop!

It is healthful to take only a few kinds of food at each meal, not to range over a large selection which causes indigestion and over-eating. Adults should not eat anything heavier than fruit before midday. That is, a heavy breakfast should not be taken. It has been proved by examination of human urine that the adult human body is cleansing itself of the by-products of the previous day's food until midday of the following day. If more food is taken, then the cleansing is checked.

One day on fruit juices or fruits only should be aimed at every week; and a laxative taken on that evening.

Any digestive upsets in pregnancy should be treated by a short fast on fruit or vegetable juices (carrot juice is especially good). A nightly laxative should then be taken. My choice of a laxative is pure senna drink. This is made by soaking an approximate ten of the large Alexandrian-type pods in a half-cup of cold water, then adding a pinch of ground ginger. The cold water and ginger method prevents griping.

I am sure that during pregnancy it is advisable to control intake of cereals, so as to prevent a heavy-boned child. The heavy bone can be made after the child is born, through the mother providing bone-building elements in her milk. I have followed this rule for myself and for the animals which I have brought through many pregnancies, and always easy birth was the result.

Abortion is a tragedy. For women who fear it, perhaps because of a previous mishap, Nature provides rock-rose to give strength to the reproductive system. Take the flowers, fresh or dried, mixed with peppermint herbal tea: a teaspoon of rock-rose flowers to every teaspoon of peppermint. 'Strength of the rock', the Gypsies say of this herb.

Also blackcurrant berries are used for actual prevention of abortion, the berries taken raw when they are in season, or preserved as a jelly, syrup, purée, etc. (*see* Recipes chapter). The fresh leaves can also be used, added to salads, or in dried form added to other herbal teas. I have saved many a cow threatening to abort, by feeding to her large amounts of blackcurrants, fruits and leaves.

All primitive people fearing difficult childbirth have their remedies to help easy labour. My personal choices, selected from the many teas, seeds and tree barks which I have seen in use, are a tea of the leaves of the wild raspberry for easy birth, a purée of blackcurrants against miscarriage, dried ginger and a pinch of gentian to prevent sickness, or a tea of peppermint and dill seed. The teas are made in the usual way, using fresh or dried herbs instead of ordinary tea. A stronger brew results if the herb is put into cold water and brought almost to the boil. Leave brew to stand until tepid. In any case, and especially in pregnancy, hot drinks should not be taken. No animal will touch liquids from which steam is still rising. We would do well to learn from them. I cannot tolerate hot food nor very cold food either.

Finally, 'man does not live by bread alone' and there is the mental side of pregnancy to be considered. The soul is great in the human body, it is mirrored in the eyes. Pregnancy is the time in the life of every woman when the soul is exceedingly powerful in her body. The soul needs food also: time should be found daily for daydreaming and reading beautiful things—which surely includes that most mystical and wonderful of all books, the Bible; and time for giving praise to God and Nature. Time must be found for care of the soul, or pregnancy will never reach its true glory.

I think pregnancy is a wonderful time because all the senses of body and mind are enhanced. Sight, scent, hearing, thought, are all more alert than normally. God and Nature arrange this. This is a time of great creativity and also great danger. Body and mind must be keen and alert to provide for and to protect the growing child, the child who may be poet or priest, general or prophet.

Legend says that women in pregnancy and childbirth have their protectors. The Holy Mother Mary is said to come in spirit to every woman who is in labour. The Greek goddess Artemis, Diana, is the protector of women in childbirth and of the newly-born infant. A group of medicinal herbs are named after her. These include the *Artemisia absinthe* (wormwood) and *Artemisia abrotanum* (southernwood), both herbs of great help in pregnancy. Wormwood gives general strength, and is highly disinfectant, it also expels worms. Its common name is 'Old Woman'. Southernwood strengthens the stomach and brain, and alleviates sickness. Its common name is 'Old Man'. Both herbs are silvery-grey of foliage. A small sprig of either one, added to the daily raspberry-leaf tea, prevents nausea. The so-called 'morning sickness' which plagues many pregnant women is mostly a body-cleansing, to protect the forming infant from the toxins resulting from faulty diet, or from nicotine (cigarette-smoking), or simply to combat the harm of over-eating, a common error in pregnancy. A few pieces of candied ginger, chewed slowly, will reduce painful vomiting, and indeed ginger is provided on many ships to combat sea-sickness. Honey is also helpful.

Before ending this chapter, which is really a mixture of practical information, odd facts collected on far travels, herbal medicine, legend, I want to say that the results of practising what I preach have been good. I personally have tested all these prescriptions for nearly twenty years (my elder child is now a healthy seventeen-year-old); and then long before, for over thirty years, I have been using these methods in veterinary work, helping animals of all kinds from mares and she-goats to the tiny miniature breeds of dogs. All those animals which had a bad

THE MOTHER

record of difficult birth-times or loss of offspring in their early
months, responded to Nature diet and herbal treatments, and
amply proved the benefits of living and working along with
Nature.

DILL (*Anethum graveolens*)

ELDER (*Sambucus nigra*)

GARLIC (*Allium sativum*)

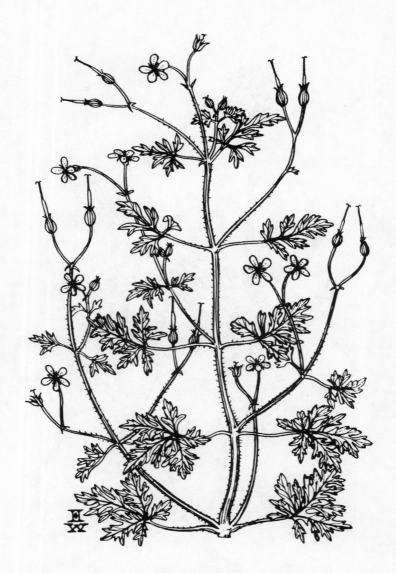

GERANIUM (*Geranium robertianum*)

2

THE FATHER

If parents will tell their children from an early age about the importance of parenthood the idea will take root in fertile soil and grow. The child can be told that people should aim at growing strong, not only for the pleasure and the power and the success in life that strength gives, but also for the good of the children who will come later in life. By far the greatest inheritance that parents can give their children is health, not money. Money is often totally lost, but good health, if simple natural rules are followed daily, remains for life, and truly can be bequeathed from parents to their offspring—so that it may even be said to last for ever.

There is little more to say, except that the father as well as the mother should try to limit indulgence in things which undermine normal health; these are alcohol, nicotine, general over-eating of unnatural foods, the use of narcotic drugs. Then there is the modern weakness of physical laziness where the taking of exercise is concerned, with resultant fat or excessively thin bodies.

A picture which I admire shows the God Pan, half-man, half-goat, running through the woods with his son, also half-child, half-goat. A goat kid gambols with them. The man's vital, laughing face and strong body, radiate joy and pride in parenthood, and the child, shaped in his image, radiates the wonder of nature-living.

There are special foods and plants which give increased physical strength to men. These are almonds, pine kernels, pomegranates, the hearts of sunflower seeds, all eaten raw, and sesame seeds, lightly roasted (the Arabs eat this seed daily with their bread and its preparation is described later), and further, that wonderful substance from flowers and fruit—honey. Black olives, and others, should be added to the list. Herbs include many members of the mint family—wild mints are the instinctive choice of bulls and stallions. Mints may be used fresh or dried—mint tea is the universal drink in Arab countries. Then there is sweet basil, used either as salad or tea. This herb was fed to the young princes of France, and in France it remains 'l'herbe royale'. Then, salep, Arabic, tha'leb, is a fine meal made from pounding sun-ripened tubers of the wild (common) orchid (*Orchis masculata*) the flour of which is made into a paste by mixing with honey. Then hot water is stirred in slowly, two dessertspoons of water to every teaspoon of the orchid flour, and then it is placed in a cup and warm milk is added to fill the cup; spices such as ground cinnamon, cloves, nutmeg, are usually added. In Turkey it is sold in the cafés as a general beverage. The fruits of the wild caper, preserved in brine, are also strengthening.

Finally the simple health rules as to diet and so forth suggested for the mother are equally valuable for the father. If the father's health fails he is unable to provide a healthy environment and good food for his family. It is poverty which crowds people into slum tenements and which puts sub-standard foods into the housewife's shopping-basket. And from that basket, unless the daily food is home-grown, comes the health of the family.

The Tibetan Buddhists say that the greatest tragedy which can befall a man is the loss of the ability to fast (disciplinary fasts are undertaken from early childhood). When a man can no longer say: 'Tomorrow I will abstain from all food or all drink, or both', and know that he will be able to do what he says, then his body is like an ancient city without walls, open wide to the enemy.

When the age for siring or bearing children is past, the cult of personal health is not so important, for then the state of a man's or woman's health does not affect the children born to them. But good health is always worth achieving.

Nor must it be forgotten that not only is health passed on from parent to child, so also are the qualities of the human soul.

3

BIRTH AND LACTATION

꽉꽉꽉

Birth, natural birth, the births of her children, are surely the greatest event in a woman's life. These births represent her immortality and the survival of the family tree for every married woman and her husband. And yet this natural act was fast becoming a time of fear, pain and repression in some stiff-ruled clinic or hospital. As countless other women have done (at least the nature-loving women) I broke away from all the shadows of clinics and hospitals for what should be a natural event, and I had my first child among Berber Arabs on a Tunisian island, and the other in the Spanish Gypsy surroundings of an old water-mill on the Sierra Nevada mountains of Andalucia. I felt the Gypsy need to be close to water and the sun and the moon; in both places I had all this, and the companionship of simple people who lived close to Nature and only understood natural childbirth.

So many women have now rebelled against unnatural ideas forced on them, that experienced doctors, meeting the demand, have written books on natural childbirth. I advise women to read these books, for many of them are excellent. They can be found in libraries the world over.

From my experience with animals of all kinds, wild and domestic, my years of careful observation in forest and field, farm and kennel, and from my personal human experiences with primitive midwives of many lands, especially the Gypsies and Arabs (who really don't have midwives at all, but a few chosen 'wise women'), I can add a little to what has been written in other published books.

Humans can always learn from the animals. The Russian

writer Mikhail Prishvin says of them: 'The animal, who knows everything, cannot talk, while man can talk, but knows very little'. I have learnt, concerning birth, something which I consider to be of first importance, that is, that animals preparing to give birth do so fasting. A consistent sign of imminent birth in animals is that they abstain from food. Some domestic animals, especially dogs, their natural instincts lost by over-long association with man, will eat immediately before birth. But the truly wild animal will not do so.

Anyone who has completed fasts, short ones or long ones, will have experienced the speedy and powerful release of energy during these fasts. At first there is sometimes 'habit hunger', but when this is overcome, and the body is released from the always heavy task of food digestion, a great flow of energy is available to be diverted to other purposes. In disease this energy is used to cure the ailment. In childbirth this energy is given to the urgent need of expelling the child, to the safe passage of the infant from the mother's womb. Food is not needed at such times, it is a hindrance only. I have spoken with women who have been given heavy meals when in the labour room of hospital and clinic, such foods as eggs, bread, soup, even meat, the usual heavy routine meals of the hospital brought to them, and eaten by them, with generally resultant pain, discomfort and vomiting.

After the birth the body is fully engaged in self-cleansing, and again has no use nor need for diversion of energy into food digestion. I fasted before and after the birth of both my children. In both cases birth was natural and easy enough. And in both cases, like the Gypsy women who give birth to their babies along the wayside and then take up the babe and follow on foot after the family wagons, I never had to stay in bed, and was bathing in the sea and river on the same day. In the case of the birth of my first child, I had to take my guard-dog Afghan hound for a walk on leash immediately after the birth, as the Berber Arabs were afraid of him and would not go near him!

Many other women known to me, following the same simple fasting rule, have felt the same strength and made the same speedy recovery from giving birth.

In more primitive times even natural-living women lost their lives in childbirth occasionally, because sometimes Nature allows

24

a misplaced child, a child which lies across the womb instead of head downwards, and the mother cannot in consequence give birth. Knowing of such danger, all women should have regular medical inspection to confirm correct position of the baby in the womb, and therefore go into labour with a calm mind, knowing that all is normal.

The Nature-birth medical books teach women to relax and let their bodies take over and act as the body dictates. I agree with this valuable advice and I had taught myself deep relaxation before my first birth-time came. I helped my spirit during labour by doing what I had seen primitive women doing during child-birth, crushing aromatic herbs in their hands and smelling them. The two herbs most used for this are coriander and verbena-scented geranium, with southernwood next in popularity. I learnt about coriander from Mexican Indians, and about verbena-geranium from the wife of the Sheikh of Djerba, my good friend. Southernwood I have seen in use among the Yemenite Jewish women.

In prolonged labour, cold cloths wrung out in a strong brew of garden mint or lavender or sage, applied cold to the temples and wrists, give pain relief and soothe the nerves, so do sips of teas made from those herbs, and from lime-blossom and rose-mary (the latter succours the heart).

When pain is acute, take drinks of poppy-heads and honey—six heads to half a pint of water, made into a tea in the usual way and sweetened with honey. In this simple form the poppy soothes—it is the 'sleep-bringer flower' not a noxious drug: the herb of drifting dreams. Pain is sent by Nature to compel the mother to work hard and fast. Fruits of rue may be chewed—nauseatingly bitter but tonic—but strong drugs should not be tolerated. Some pain is natural, even exciting, part of the mystical experience. The child too helps in the effort, and drugs could make him into a heavy burden. The peace after pain is sweet and worth waiting for.

When complications occur, a strong brew of raspberry leaves should be given, and this brew should be kept ready-made in case it is needed. This herb helps in the actual birth effort. Also a restorative drink of spiced wine (but nothing stronger) may be given: this wine is made by pounding up a mixture of equal parts of cloves, cinnamon and candied ginger, and adding a dessert-spoon of this mixture to every pint of sweet wine.

Rock-rose is powerful in 'shock' treatment. Indeed this herb is in common use amongst herbalists for giving to victims of car accidents, work accidents, etc.

Juice from crushed elder leaves or blossoms dropped into the mouth and massaged into the temples will hold faintness at bay.

Essence of red roses (a few drops in water) is also effective. Another proven restorative is spirits of lavender, applied to nostrils, temples and wrists, also about six drops can be taken internally on a lump of sugar (*see* Recipes chapter).

In cases of retained after-birth, first try strong dosages of raspberry leaves; if not successful, add a teaspoon of crushed ivy leaves to every two teaspoons of raspberry leaves, make into a tea sweetened with honey, and take a strong laxative such as Epsom salts or castor oil or a draught from fourteen senna pods.

Immediately after the birth of my first child, the Arab negress helping me trampled my abdominal area with her supple brown feet. She explained that it was 'to put the body back into shape'. I could understand the reason for this massage, and I think that some such massage should be given, also cold-water baths, which I sought instinctively and which primitive women take.

The importance of fresh air during labour must be stressed, and that is one of the aids which clinics and hospitals are seldom able to provide. The boon of sleep should not be forgotten; it is the best after-childbirth restorative—a quiet, deep, untroubled sleep, with the new-born infant sweet after a first bath in herb-scented water (rose petals, lavender and rosemary tops, jasmine, sage, geranium, meadowsweet—any or several of these), at the mother's side, not isolated in some hospital baby-ward! That is what all the female animals do after they have given birth; without having eaten or taken liquids, they go to sleep for a long session. During sleep their first milk arrives, and then begins the important aftermath of birth and the beginning of the making of a healthy infant, lactation.

Lactation is such a simple thing for the primitive woman, that it is a common sight to see Gypsy women in the market-places, walking around, supporting with one hand a babe feeding at the breast, and with the other hand offering bunches of herbs for sale.

I am not going to write about the technicalities of breast-feeding. This information can be obtained from parent or nurses (if the babe is born in hospital or clinic) or, if preferred, from medical books. I will write instead about the nature-lore on breast-feeding, which I have obtained from many lands. Breast-feeding should not begin for the infant until at least twelve hours after birth. I have noted that the first aim of women who always make a success of breast-feeding, is to keep the baby healthy and contented, for a strongly sucking child is a necessity for full milk production in both animal and man.

Nipples are anointed with pleasant things, to prevent soreness and cracking, and also to be an attraction for the feeding baby. Thin honey, almond oil, rose-water, buttermilk, are usually applied. Any areas of inflammation of nipples or breast are treated by cooling applications of such things as cucumber (raw, crushed to a pulp), a thick lotion of cooked bran, cold buttermilk, or extract of witch-hazel, or a pack of sorrel or violet leaves.

It is also fully accepted that there can be no fixed rules for feeding times. The needs of every babe are different. Only it is considered better not to night-feed, better for both mother and child to sleep when all the world is sleeping except for the nocturnal creatures—many of them evil—and man is not nocturnal.

Nature people live far from shops and pharmacies; they do not expect to feed their children on dried milk products imbibed from a glass bottle shaped to resemble a human breast. Therefore they give much thought and care to milk production. They know well that the mother's milk is best, but failing that they will use milk from the milch animals.

It is accepted that plentiful sleep and the taking of liquids increase milk production. The following foods and plants are proved to help make milk. First the cereals, especially oats, barley, maize, all taken raw, the oats in flaked form, taken with milk, the barley soaked in water for two days to soften, and then eaten with a little salt or honey or maple syrup, the maize eaten when very newly ripe and milky, direct from the cob—when fresh maize is not available then make corn mash, by cooking the ground corn (meal) like rice. (*See* Recipes chapter.)

All the onion family: the onions enrich the milk and give antiseptic properties; steamed leeks are very good.

All the pulses, broad beans, peas, lima beans, can be eaten raw when fresh and tender, otherwise, cook in very little water with a teaspoon of lemon juice and a pinch of salt added to every large cup of the pulses. Lentils are valuable, soaked overnight, can also be eaten raw, minced; so can chick peas, which are sweet-tasting.

All raw fruits, especially apples, pears, grapes, peaches, bananas. All the berries, especially blackcurrants and rose hips. The citrus fruits are the least helpful, as too much will decrease the amount of milk.

Root vegetables, especially carrots, sweet potatoes and parsnips. Common potatoes are sometimes fermentative, and turnips and swedes make the milk strong-tasting and therefore objectionable to the infant feeding.

Of all the plants, all the green herbs, especially wild garlic leaves, spring onions, sage, milk thistle, comfrey, chicory, mallow, dill, coriander, borage (borage, flowers and young leaves, is one of the best milk producers) and all the clovers also are very good, eaten in the salad, likewise dandelion leaves, watercress, landcress, alfalfa (lucerne), melilot, milkwort. Fennel is an important galactogogue, having an immediate influence on increase of milk; leaves, stems, seeds are all used.

All nuts, especially walnut, almond, pistachio and chestnut.

All seeds are good, including especially sunflower, sesame, fenugreek, linseed, celery, carrot, anise, onion and poppy.

A milk-productive beverage is made by adding powdered sesame seed to sweet red wine (as much seed as can be tolerated), or adding the mashed, inner parts of baked egg plant to the wine.

It is an error to say that a nursing mother must take milk from animals to increase her own milk. Remember the abundant milk yield of dairy cows, goats and other milch animals, all produced on a purely vegetarian diet. Nursing mothers may drink some milk, but should not overdo it, remembering that it creates mucus. Better to take juicy berries. Good air is also important for milk production; fresh, moving air coming through open windows and the oxygen derived from ample outdoors exercise taken daily. Notable is the abundance of milk produced by women living close to the earth as contrasted with that of women living cooped up in city apartments. One of the worst inventions of modern times is finewire mesh nailed over windows in an attempt to keep out flies, mosquitoes and other small insects (which are increasing in our era, mainly because the birds and larger insects which preyed upon them have been destroyed by poison-spraying of agricultural land.)

Far better and more natural to sleep with open windows, or altogether outdoors as my family do except at times of rain or really bitter cold, and to apply a herbal lotion to the skin if biting insects are around. A recipe for a herbal midge and mosquito lotion, easy to make and good for the human skin, can be found in my book, *Herbal Handbook for Everyone* (London, 1966), on pages 21 and 148.

Finally it should be said that a primitive woman usually expects to breast-feed her child for two years, or even longer, unless she becomes pregnant, and then will not feed after the fourth month of pregnancy.

But total failure of milk, through accident or other unexpected causes, must be considered. The most natural thing to do then is to find a human foster-mother. This was quite commonly done in former times. It was then a quite usual thing for rich women to hand over their babies to so-called 'wet-nurses', to have them breast-fed for a half year, in the mistaken belief that they would keep their own breasts shapely and unspoilt, whereas breast-feeding of infants develops the breasts and increases their beauty. The only exception to this is when women take on the feeding of many infants at one time, as is still done among many Beduin tribes where young mothers are working far away from the Black Tents of their tribes, and one older woman, who has borne a child, remains at home and suckles the infants of as many as six other women.

Milch animals are sometimes used to foster human babies, animals such as goat, ewe, ass or mare, and in some regions, reindeer. The goat is the best for the human baby, ewes being timid and asses and mares more uncertain-tempered when so used. Goat's milk is very digestible, primarily because the fat globules are integrated in the milk, and not gathered into 'top' milk. This milk is rich in calcium, fluorine and phosphorus. It is far superior to cow's milk for children as it possesses similar consistency to mother's milk and is of similar chemical analysis.

Cow's milk is the most commonly used for human infants because it is the most convenient. However, it should be remembered that the constituents of cow's milk are such that this milk will raise a mature heifer within one year, and no one can compare the size and build of a heifer to those of a human child of one year of age!

The only drawback with goats is that they are over clever and therefore often rebellious and difficult to manage (it is said that they only willingly accept orders from the Devil!). They lack the placidity of the typical cow. The more manageable breeds of goats are the Toggenburg, Nubian and Syrian Damascus.

Personal experience is always interesting and valuable. My first child I breast-fed with ease for nearly a year and a half, when continuing far travels made weaning necessary. My second child was deprived of my milk from the early age of two months, through accident. The story is told in my book *Spanish Mountain Life*, about the early years and months of my children in the company of peasants and Gypsies of the Sierra Nevada region near Granada, Spain. The book is out of print, but can be found in many libraries.

My second child was fed as already described in this Nature book. She first had a foster-mother, a young Spanish Gypsy friend who had borne a son a short time before the birth of my daughter. She fed my daughter for two months until the demands of her son left insufficient milk for a foster-child, and then I chose as a new foster-mother the goat from the water-mill where we were living.

The method of using a milch animal is as follows. Before the human baby is held to the udder, the udder is cleansed of dust, etc., with a clean, water-dampened cloth. The baby is then rubbed against the goat (or other animal) to get the scent of the foster-mother, before being put to suckle. The baby is fed in the same way as if at the human mother's breast, alternating teats, and being helped to empty the breasts.

The goat is led to the baby's cradle at regular feeding times. The goat that I used for my daughter would come home herself from pasture, to stand by the cradle and offer her udder. The animal had a wonderful sense of hours, and loved the human baby as if a kid of her own. When the time came for me to leave Spain to attend to veterinary work awaiting me in England, I wanted to take the goat with me, but I was refused agricultural permits for a Spanish goat to enter England.

Many people around us on the Sierra Nevada had been raised on goats, and they all looked very strong. Indeed they told me that one of the foremost boxers of the region had been goat-reared. They also said that goat-reared people were invariably noble of character!

In Spain a legend relates (it is found in the school-books there), that the Milky Way of the stars is goat's milk, a dripping from the udder of a fabulous goat which had been chosen to foster the only prince of a kingdom whose mountains touched the heavens. The infant prince was lost when the king took him on a hunting trip. The goat would not allow anyone to milk her, and ran off in search of the prince. Eventually she found him and saved his life with the milk she had held back for him, much of which had dripped from her bursting udder as she searched. The king later strewed diamonds along the 'way of milk' and this accounts for the bright stars seen there.*

The healthy and hardy wandering Bedouin Arabs, true children of Nature, understand from their close kinship with animals how much better it is for the human infant to find a human foster-mother or milch animal if the mother's own milk fails. This

---

* In my long novel, *Look! The Wild Swans* (C. W. Daniel) I describe the saving of a baby by his half-sister. The baby, considered as dead, had been put in the goat-shed, covered with a piece of blanket. The half-sister, although very young, had been sensible and responsible enough to carry the baby to a goat that had suckled him. This novel about the Snowdon mountain region of Wales was written nearly ten years before the birth of my daughter, and I had forgotten this episode at the time when the Spanish people suggested the goat as foster-mother during my own drama. My family on my father's side came from Toledo before their journey to Turkey at the time of the Inquisition, so such an event may have been in my family's past. It may account for my devotion to animals, especially to goats and the Afghan hounds which somewhat resemble them. My novel has long been out of print and has been classified as a 'rare book'; but in England in 1967 nearly a thousand copies were found and it is therefore still obtainable from De Baïracli Levy, Blissford, Fordingbridge, Hants.

provision means milk of a natural and regular warmth in place of the differing temperatures of fire-heated substitute milk, and from a soft udder in place of a glass bottle and rubber teat (both difficult to keep truly clean). Animal udders can be washed easily, and the teats wiped with a clean cloth at every feeding time. The Beduins also recognize the influence of milk on the feeding infant. They have told me, for example, that when young goats are brought up on foster ewes, their hair becomes softer, and when lambs are fostered by goats, the lambs'-wool becomes coarser. Therefore it is possible that when the popular modern food for infants, dried milk, is used, and no one knows from what cows the milk has come, the baby so reared gets milk from numerous cows, and this creates disturbances in the emotions (and stomach) of the infant.

The local doctor of the Sierra Nevada had tried to persuade me to use dried milk for my baby. I had agreed to give her some supplementary feeds of this form of milk, but when I was mixing it, and saw how tightly the milk-water mixture adhered to cup and spoon, I realized that the unnatural substance would likewise be gluing itself to the baby's delicate digestive tract, and I refused to give further feeds of such a food.

Families living in city apartments of course cannot use milch animals for their infants, and nowadays human foster-mothers cannot be found. Therefore if bottled goat's milk is not obtainable, then cow's milk will have to be used. Try then for T.T. Jersey milk, which may not be pasteurized.

If pasteurized, then a tablespoon of water-soaked, flaked barley or oats should be added to the milk for extra vitality and vitamins. Soak the flaked cereal overnight in tepid water (enough to cover the cereal lightly), then press out the liquid the following morning and add to the milk. Also add a half-teaspoon of pure honey to every tablespoon of the cereals liquid.

Sips of fresh fruit juice should be given in between the milk feeds to replace the vitamin C, etc., lost in the pasteurizing. Canned and bottled fruit juices have no place in a true Nature diet.

I prefer feeding with a cup and teaspoon, to the glass bottle. I have reared many kinds of young creatures using cup and spoon. This method prevents the greedy gulping and over-feeding common with bottle-feeding, and the pain of the indigestion which follows.

I have spoon-fed such creatures as young owls (which grew up to healthy adulthood able to live in freedom amongst other owls) as well as children of others. I never weighed my children either at birth or later. They would be far smaller and lighter than children whose mothers eat large quantities of food during pregnancy and who themselves receive fattening supplementary foods from an early age. Scales would have told me nothing of any value.

Babies should be fed in peaceful surroundings and at leisure; tension is rapidly communicated to them. Loud voices, adult conversation, noise of radios are inimical to successful breast-feeding. The quietly humming voice of the mother, or the rustle of wind-stirred leaves and grasses, bring tranquillity and health to the baby.

Visitors are disturbing until the infant is at least one month old. Animals always try to hide their young away during the early weeks.

4

THE INFANT

Concerning the care of the infant I learnt much from people who cannot write nor read books, wandering people mostly, and therefore some of the information which I now give should be original.

I have already written about the first bath of the new-born babe. I think that in the same way that women find time to knit or sew infant clothes during pregnancy, they should also take time to gather and dry flowers for the baths of the coming infant, also to gather and dry herbs for treatment of minor ailments which may occur.

Sweet scents give strength. For instance during the strenuous Arabian fast of Ramadan, believers are not permitted to enjoy the scent of flowers, as the perfume lessens the severity of the fast.

For my first-born I gathered and dried quantities of the incredibly sweet-scented small pink roses of Tunisia, and the carnations of heavier scent, and the white jasmine. For my daughter I had wild 'May' blossom (the hawthorn) from the hills, and orange and lemon blossom, and the noted giant jasmine of Granada, which I asked Gypsy friends to keep for me. They wear bunches of this flower to give them strength whilst dancing.

The baby's eyes should be cleansed with a soothing brew made from poppy flowers or fruits and lavender flowers—a teaspoon of both, to every cup of water. The rest of the body should be bathed in the flower-scented, tepid water. Hot water should only be used if the baby is really dirty, otherwise never go above tepid heat, and finish off with a cool splash. Running water is the best thing to use for the final rinse. It was a law of the Essene sect of the Dead Sea Scrolls, who so well understood the natural laws of health, that bathing must be performed in running water.

A very good cleansing aid is an oatmeal bag (*see* page 76).

Faces, hands, and other areas which get more dirty than the rest of the body, in between baths, can be cleansed with swabs of cotton wool dampened with water and then sprinkled with herbal oils made by heating aromatic herbs such as lavender, rosemary, thyme, sage, in natural oils with a small amount of vinegar added: an approximate dessertspoon to a pint of oil. Heat used can be that of the sun or a warm oven. I never used soap on my children's faces. Any skin soreness, especially winter chapping from cold winds, can be cured speedily by applying almond oil, or almond oil mildly diluted with rose-water, a teaspoon of rose-water to every tablespoon of the oil.

I think that the infant should be trained almost from birth to excrete into a receptacle, and not to lie on its back and soil itself. Only the child of man and the offspring of the pig and rodents soil themselves. As I write this book in an old stone house in Upper Galilee, Israel, I have before me an example of infant cleanliness given by the young swallows living inside my house. (I have a swallows' nest in every room, and five nests in the room in which I am writing this book.) Every nest is organized in the same way. From an early age the swallow chicks sleep with their tails over the nests: a row of little swallows, each with its tail outside the nest, carefully excreting on to the floor below where I have placed pieces of wood to collect their dirt for my rose-bushes! I find such a small matter as the cleanliness of young swallows really notable—the careful planning of Nature.

It takes much time and patience to train an infant not to soil itself, but it is very worthwhile and saves much time later on. The baby will usually excrete on waking from sleep and after meals, therefore he should be held over a chamber pot at these times. Urination is, of course, more difficult to control, being more frequent and irregular in timing, and infants cannot be trained to be dry. I used to pad my children's diapers with sheets of absorbent paper or with old soft cloths which I could burn, and whenever possible they lay in the cradle without wearing napkins, bedded on that absorbent herb, sphagnum moss. In World War II, using my huge Irish wolfhound as a sort of 'pack-horse', I brought sackloads of sphagnum moss down from the boggy places of Exmoor, and dried it and despatched it to the British Army using this moss for wound dressings.

In their study of the American Indian, in their rare paper on American Indian plant medicine and food, the New York unit of the Herb Society of America describes sphagnum moss as follows: 'Sphagnum moss (*Sphagnum cymbidium*) to line papoose's cradle, antiseptic and absorbent.'

This common moss of damp or boggy places dries to feather weight and will absorb a tremendous amount of moisture. It was in common use in old wars and its use was recorded during the Scottish Highland wars.

Berber Arabs use a sheepskin, woolly side uppermost, to place beneath babies in the cradle; this can be washed easily and dries speedily. As a vegetarian I could not use a sheepskin for my children.

Powdered orris root (of fragrant scent), or powdered oats (fine oatmeal) or common talcum powder should be dusted between the legs to prevent skin-chafing.

For maximum health the infant needs more than a daily water bath as time goes by. After one month, air and sun baths should be taken. Both kinds of bath should be short at first. Air baths are taken by an open window at the warmest hours of the day, around midday, by merely letting the infant lie naked in the cradle, beginning with five minutes and increasing to one hour within the month. Of course airbathing is not possible during winter or cold spells.

Sunbathing depends on the time of the year. In winter duration must be short, and in hot climates also short, and the infant's head and feet must always be shaded. The feet, not the head, should point towards the sun. The ideal sunbathing place for an infant is secure in a cradle beneath a leafy tree. The breeze moving the tree foliage gives and takes the sunlight and prevents burning.

It is beneficial to rub the skin lightly with oil, before exposure to the sun. (Use herbal oils as previously described for cleansing the skin.) If the heavy olive oil is used, it especially needs to be thinned down with a little vinegar, a half-teaspoon to a tablespoon of this oil. The Romans thought so highly of olive oil for skin-health, that they habitually carried oil flasks attached to their belts. Julius Caesar (and I mention this elsewhere) was convinced of the beneficial effects of both olive oil and honey.

Sunburn must be avoided; remember that infant skin is very tender. Never risk a sun bath for an infant unless watch can be kept all the time to prevent burning (this needs the same watchfulness as rice cooking in the pot!). But if burning does occur, apply fresh cucumber juice, and when not available milk with a very little liquid honey added—goat's milk is especially good—or buttermilk and honey, or dock leaves laid over the place (*see* 'Sunburn' in Nature Medicine chapter).

Eye-bathing has already been described on the first page of this chapter. It is as important as body-bathing, especially in dusty areas and in towns. The great Arabian doctor, Avicenna, advised bathing the infant's eyes (and body) twice daily.

For sore eyes make a brew of marshmallow flowers and roots. This contains a soothing and healing mucilage: one handful of flowers and a tablespoon of the root washed and finely sliced, to a pint of water. Bathe the eyes with this. Anoint the lids with almond oil and rosewater, but do not let this enter the eyes.

The navel cord area should have some antiseptic treatment, and the best application is extract of witch-hazel, on swabs of cotton-wool previously dampened in water. If any soreness occurs use the same soothing lotion of mallow flowers and roots as advised for the eyes. Any festering should be treated with fresh rosemary pounded up (it is an evergreen herb), placed over the area, and some fresh leaves such as elder, lettuce, geranium, violet, placed over this as bandage, and over all a cotton cloth bound to hold the leaves in place.

Very young animals and human infants possess powerful resistance to disease, and a young baby usually keeps healthy for at least its first few months of life—and for ever after if naturally reared. Nevertheless, later in this chapter I shall give natural treatments for a few minor ailments.

The first few weeks have their difficulties, if not health problems. For this is the period in which the baby has to adjust itself to the new way of life outside the mother's sheltering womb. When this time is past, the infant usually sleeps from mealtime to mealtime. Therefore, in the first weeks the conditions of the womb should be imitated. The infant's quarters should be kept shady, no glare of sun or electric light allowed. There should also be shelter from harsh sounds. If a rocking cradle can be provided, this resembles the motion that the baby knew when carried to and fro within the womb, the rocking motion of the mother's moving body when she was awake.

Now comes the all-important subject of the feeding of the infant, for on good food in its early months depends the whole future health of the individual.

The League of Nations' Interim Report on the 'Problem of Nutrition', although published many years ago, will always be applicable. The report stated:

'Viewing the nutrition question as a whole, however, the greatest emphasis deserves to be laid on one particular aspect, namely nutrition of children. Only by adequate nutrition in the earliest years of life can the health and full development of the future citizen be assured. Pregnant women, nursing mothers, infants and young children, must be considered from a nutritional standpoint as the most vulnerable portion of the community, in the sense that damage inflicted in childhood by bad food cannot be subsequently repaired.'

That is why I think that the mother should spare no trouble nor self-discipline to make good milk for the infant which is dependent upon her. In the previous chapter I have written about lactation and the production of an abundance of breast-milk, and have also written about substitutes for mother's milk.

It is a mistake to be dogmatic about the hours of infant feeding. These must differ with the individual babe, and are even affected by climate and time of year. But basically babies need to be fed at four-hourly intervals, beginning at early dawn, and not fed at all during the night (at least only sips of herbal teas should be given if the infant cries and seems thirsty. The human race is not nocturnal. Night is a time of rest for body and brain and stomach, and the human infant should abide by this life rhythm.)

More frequent meals should be given when the infant is newly born, and especially when living in a hot climate. Suggested times are: from birth to two months: three-hourly feeds, beginning at 6 a.m. and ending at 9 p.m. Then from two months onwards, four-hourly feeds, ending at 8 p.m. Water may be offered at all times, plain or in the form of herbal teas.

It is a mistake to withhold water, saying that it is unnatural for babies. From an early age the young of all animals, even the carnivores such as fox and wolf cubs, lick up dew and snow, and certainly the young of herbivores are eager for such moisture in addition to their mother's milk.

The mother should use her intelligence to provide cool drinks for the infant, especially when the weather is hot and dry. The Arabs stressed this to me for my child, and I soon realized that they knew what they were talking about.

A few drops of lemon in a half-wineglass of water, fed by teaspoon, are cleansing and refreshing, and the drink is improved by the addition of a half-teaspoon of pure honey. Berry juices make rich blood and provide vitamins and minerals, especially raspberry, blackberry, loganberry and all the currants. Gooseberries are too strong for the infant. The juices should be given undiluted with water, except during illness, when some mild dilution is preferable. Pomegranate is one of the most refreshing and nerve-soothing drinks, but needs dilution, half in half with water. Other than lemon, the citrus fruits should not be given in the early months.

As I have written, food needs differ greatly with the individual infant. Some need more than the usual amounts, some need less. It is the baby's own desires which must be studied and granted. Only the rule of no night breast-feeds should be enforced.

When an infant refuses food, then let it sleep instead. Natural appetite will return as surely as the dawn comes with each new day.

The mother should hand-milk away any milk which the infant does not consume, in order to prevent damage to her breasts through congestion.

If a baby appears unsatisfied with its food then give more, until he is satisfied, and if there is no more milk to give, then it may be necessary to supplement with other milk from goat or cow. Only, as I have said earlier in this book, if such milk must be used let it be as natural as possible, do not give dried milk and do not boil fresh milk.

For an infant not sufficiently robust, an excellent easily digested and very strengthening nut milk can be given. This drink I learnt of from the Arabs. Sweet almonds are blanched by pouring hot water over them to remove the skins. The white kernels are pounded in a mortar and to each dessertspoon of the liquid are added two dessertspoons of water at blood heat. This is left to stand for several hours in a warm place, then the milky liquid is fed to the infant, two teaspoons to a meal with a half-teaspoonful of honey. The mother should eat the residue in the mortar.

Ailments of the infant generally are few, when nature-reared. Possible minor ailments are: feverishness, diarrhoea, threadworms, skin irritation.

Fevers in early age are treated by: giving lemon-water first thing in the early morning, giving all the fruit juice and water mixture that the baby will take, before putting to the breast, especially making use of the blood-cooling berries, such as raspberries, strawberries, mulberries and cactus fruits juice. Give chamomile tea, an accepted fever tea for infants even with the orthodox. Sips of buttermilk can also be given. Reduce duration of the breast feeds until the fever subsides. A water enema may have to be given if the fever is prolonged; as fever tends to dry up the bowels. To give the enema, an infant's bulb-type syringe is used. The nozzle should not be longer than an inch and a half, and should be lubricated with oil. Two to four ounces of plain tepid water are enough for the infant under four months of age. To give the enema, first expel a few drops of the water to drive out the air. The baby should now be placed on its back, and the legs held against the chest. Then the nozzle is inserted gently into the anus using a screwlike turning action, and the water should be emptied into the bowel, until two or three ounces have been received. Four ounces is the maximum for an infant under six months. Diarrhoea is treated by a fast on water and lemon for twenty-four hours. Then treat as for fever, and if the diarrhoea persists, an enema should be given. Also, for persistent infant diarrhoea, spiced barley water can be given before breastfeeds, and that is made by scalding barley grain and then letting it stand for twelve hours. Use a cupful of barley to one and a half pints of hot water. Now pour through a fine-mesh sieve, and press the barley well to extract all the moisture. To the resultant liquid add a pinch of finely-powdered ginger, nutmeg and cinnamon.

All these spices are warming and antiseptic. Also helpful is the Spanish peasant remedy of plasters over the abdomen. Leaves of celery are placed in a thick layer on warmed flannel, a dampened piece of flannel is then placed over, and all is bound in place by a cotton cloth. Elder-tree foliage can replace the celery when this is not obtainable.

In very prolonged dysentery, fast on tepid dill-water: only a teaspoon of dill seed made into a tea in a cupful of cold water which is then heated to just below boiling point. After twenty-four to forty-eight hours of fasting on dill-water, feed the infant a Nature Gruel before breast-feeds. Nature Gruel is made to my own formula, and was originally evolved for the use of young or orphaned animals, for their weaning and their rearing (please see page 99 for a further mention). But this gruel is also a well-tried remedy for all kinds of digestive disorders. The American (Red) Indian discovery of the properties of the inner bark of the Slippery (Red) elm tree, which forms an internal poultice as well as being very strengthening, has been made use of in the formula; the slippery elm is a basic ingredient.

The gruel is given mixed with honey and milk, and full instructions are supplied with the product. Both my children were weaned on this gruel, and it has also been used medicinally for years by myself and other mothers preferring natural remedies.

Another helpful herb is yarrow, given as a tea. Infants sometimes have ear ailments, which are really only the result of a cleansing process of the body following birth. The ears should be soothed by dropping into both a small teaspoon of a brew of red rose petals, made in the same way as dill-water. Treat both ears even if only one is painful. Poppy-heads can be used instead. Use from four to six fresh or dried wild poppy fruits to a large cup of water. Again make as for dill-water, but allow to steep in the water for several hours. Steeping means letting the herbs stand in the heated water, covered, and without straining. Use the rose or poppy lotion tepid, pouring a teaspoon into both ears, massaging very gently, then drying out with dampened swabs of cotton-wool wound around tweezers.

Skin irritation sometimes occurs soon after birth, and again is a cleansing process. Make a brew of lavender flowers or elder blossom, as described for poppy, steeping well. Apply this, on cotton cloths, as cold packs to the affected area. Then massage the area deeply to stimulate blood circulation in the affected parts. Napkin rashes should be soothed with swabs of water-dampened cotton wool sprinkled with witch-hazel extract. Then the sore place should be dusted with powdered herbs or talcum powder. Other herbs to soothe chafed infant skin are the wonderfully cooling lotions made from bean flowers, crushed strawberries, vine leaves, goats' milk and from the flowers of madonna lilies (which all reads like a poem!).

Scurf cap on the head should be treated by morning and night friction with a lotion made from common cold tea (the tannic acid in the tea being the reason for its use) or with a strong brew made from the silvery and scented sprays of meadowsweet flowers—four or five sprays of meadowsweet to one and a half pints of water. The mother should also help the baby through her milk supply, by eating an abundance of raw green foods, especially watercress and turnip-tops. The mother can also lightly cook young nettles and eat them once a day (when they are in season).

A protruding navel, which shows as a small rupture, should be treated in its early stages by placing a flat pebble over the place, covering with a piece of lint, and keeping in place with adhesive tape. Morning and night the pebble should be removed for a short while, and the area massaged with a good astringent such as a strong brew of ivy leaves, a tablespoon of finely cut-up ivy leaves to two cups of water, made into a brew by simmering for about ten minutes, and then steeping for several hours.

Screaming bouts are usual in infants, and the stronger the infant the louder the noise! Daily screaming bouts for a quarter-hour or so are a form of lung exercise for many infants, and do not indicate indigestion or ill-health or anger! If the screaming continues all day or all night then the cause must be ascertained, and the infant soothed by giving sips of dill-seed tea with honey, or drops of rose-water in plain water (a teaspoon of rose-water to a cup of plain water). A cotton cloth dipped in a strong brew of garden mint and applied to the head and to the back of the neck, is also helpful to calm an unduly screaming infant.

Teething of course is not an ailment but some infants have tough gums and therefore suffer pain. It is the double teeth which may give trouble. The baby should be soothed with a warm drink of poppy-heads tea and honey, four or five poppy heads to a cup of water, or a drink of lime-blossom tea before sleeping. Also if the weather is cold, a hot-water bottle (I prefer a fire-heated stone wrapped up in cloths) put in the cot helps to comfort the baby. A crying infant should be taken to sleep in its mother's bed. Rubbing the gums with oil of cloves is warming and helpful.

Vomiting. Even the healthiest of infants will sometimes vomit up a little food, especially when feeding greedily. Wash out the mouth with tepid water to which a few drops of lavender water have been added, ten drops to two tablespoons of water. Give the infant sips of dill-water. If vomiting is continual, then fast from all food and treat as for fever.

(For minor ailments of the older child see Nature Medicine chapter, page 63.)

Sleep treatment is very important, as the new-born infant spends most of the first months of its life outside the womb in sleep. A rocking cradle is ideal, and should be made of wood if possible. Bedclothes should be light, loose, and all cotton. If woollen covers are chosen, they must be top covers only. Avoid nylon and plastics. As both my children were born in areas of snakes and scorpions, I always kept protective aromatic herbs bunched in their cradles, especially rue, rosemary and sage. But even if there are no such dangers, such herbs are a pleasant addition to an infant's cradle, hung in bunches and tucked under the cot mattress.

If a pillow is given it should be a flat unfilled one. The infant should lie with the abdomen downwards, preferably, or on its right side. Sleeping on the left side should be discouraged, or only allowed for short intervals. Also, preferably, the feet should point East or North for healthful cosmovital vibrations. Before sleep all excitement should be avoided, and surrounding quietness should prevail. Even in cold winter months a window must always be left open, the wider the better. If night-time heating of the bedroom is needed, then try to provide wood or coal as fuel, and avoid oil heaters.

Infants' clothing should be all cotton or linen, and loosely fitting. Avoid synthetic fabrics. In very cold weather a woollen top-jacket can be worn. But the ideal for child-health is the

Gypsy babe, rolling naked, like a wolf cub, in the snow. Head covering should not press on the ears tightly, the best model being the conical hood attached to coat (burnoose) of the North African Arab. Footwear should be round-toed and loose.

There are some dangers from animals during the early months of an infant's life. Although such dangers are rare, parents should know of them, and never leave a young infant unprotected and vulnerable to animal dangers. Cats have been known to seek warmth from an infant, and if lying on the child's face can cause death from smothering. Eagles, which sometimes prey on young lambs and goat kids, carrying them off in their talons, can attack countryside babies. In Djerba, the Tunisian island where my first child was born, the negress helper, a wise and wonderful woman who had been with me for the birth, insisted that I barred up the high window of the small Berber Arab house where my baby was born and sometimes had to be left alone. Babies on that island had been attacked by great birds. And when I was living in Granada, Spain, in the mid nineteen-fifties, I well remember the death of a baby attacked by rats when the mother stayed away overlong shopping. In one of London's well-known maternity homes a baby suffered from facial disfigurement caused by mice. In a forestry area in England where I worked in World War II, many of the workers in the hostel where we slept were bitten on ears and nose by mice when they were in a deep sleep after hard manual work. Therefore such dangers are real, and one of the best safeguards against them is to have a family dog as guard over the human family. My children had Afghan hounds guarding them from their infancy to teenage years.

The infant must be constantly in the parents' thoughts during the first nine months of its life, for this is the time of intense development, similar to the nine months of growth within the womb. The babe grows from infant into child during that time, and then is able to show some independence of his mother: now he is able to travel short distances by crawling, and some freedom of thought is also shown. A nine-months child can control its excreta, and clothing and bedding will remain almost clean; control of urine takes longer and is rarely developed before one year is reached and often not until much later.

It should be realized that within those eighteen months, nine within the womb and nine feeding at the mother's breast, the whole basis of the future of the child is forged. And good health is the true rich inheritance which parents can bequeath to their children and which by a hundredfold surpasses mere money riches. A healthy soul needs to grow in a healthy body, and man is body and flesh, soul and spirit.

Having ensured that the infant is well fed and gets enough sleep, provision for its other needs must be arranged, and therefore from an early age communion with nature should be taught. The baby should be lifted up to see the sun by day and the moon and stars by night. I have always tried to live in places where no person could pass in front of my windows, and therefore it was not necessary to curtain out the moon and stars. Moonlight has much power to give and it seems to me intolerable that mankind, from mere convention, should shut out moonlight from human lives. My chosen people, the Gypsies, make all possible use of moonlight in their constant search for good health (W. H. Hudson, author and naturalist, said of the Gypsies that he had never met any one of them suffering from a cold, or headache or indigestion; that they could live outdoors the year round under conditions which would have killed off less hardy people, and could eat food, including carrion, which no other people could digest). Whenever possible the Gypsies pass their nights outdoors: and I arranged this for my children. From birth onwards my infant son slept out beneath the brilliant Tunisian moon.

Infant hands should be raised and lowered to touch trees and flowers; and wild birds and animals should be pointed out; all these things are a child's inheritance.

My son grew up near a pomegranate tree growing in the courtyard. Every day as a sort of rite he was held against the tree to touch it. We saw the orange-red flame-coloured bell flowers open, and we watched the fruit forming rounded and good. Only we were leaving the Tunisian island long before the proper ripening of the pomegranates; we were leaving in July and the pomegranates were harvested in September and later. However, one fruit on our tree grew apace, and on the day we were due to leave for France, the fruit looked so round and complete that I decided to pick it and to open it. The pomegranate proved to be lusciously ripe: a gift from the tree. The island Berbers remembered very well for a long time that strange out-of-season ripening of the pomegranate.

GORSE (*Ulex europaeus*)

MEADOWSWEET (*Filipendula ulmaria*)

MARSH MALLOW (*Althea officinalis*)

PRIMROSE (*Primula vulgaris*)

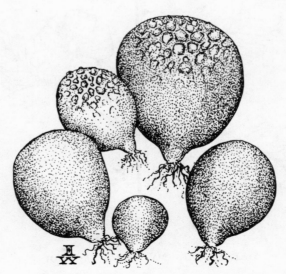

PUFFBALL FUNGAE (Genus *Lycoperdon*)

5

THE CHILD

꙳꙳꙳꙳

The change-over from infancy to childhood is a slow process and passes almost unnoticed. The main difference really is that formerly all nourishment was taken by sucking; this is now complemented by chewing and biting.

After the first two teeth have appeared breast-milk diet should be fortified with other simple and easily digested foods such as prepared fruit and vegetable juices and cereals. Dentition is troublesome for most babies and their parents. Good teeth are not nowadays everybody's birthright, and it requires many generations of a well-balanced and natural diet to ensure good teeth in a family.

Hungarian research workers in human dentition took a great interest in the Gypsy population of the region, because their teeth were noticeably excellent. It was found that not a single case of artificial feeding of Gypsy infants was known, that the Gypsy children were often breast-fed up to the age of four and five years, and that breast-feeding was a precondition of proper calcification and development of teeth. Doctors K. Balogh and G. Huszar found that Gypsies have exceptionally fine teeth, far healthier than those of non-Gypsies. Then Rumanian researchers Uleia and Baculescu Pascu observed that the dentition of wandering Gypsies living in primitive conditions is better than that of non-Gypsies of the same localities, and also noted that old Gypsy women had especially good teeth despite the large families born to them, averaging eight infants. Many modern doctors are opposed to over-long breast-feeding, and it used often to be the practice only because the nursing

47

mother wished to avoid pregnancy. Of this, more will be said later.

The teething of infants has been mentioned in the previous chapter. With nature-reared babies there should be no difficulties and certainly none of the complications so common with orthodox rearing, where teething often brings on convulsions, ear disorders and even epilepsy!

In infancy the dominant interest of the babe was, as we have seen, to be sucking when not sleeping, and this interest gives place in early childhood to chewing and biting. Everything within reach is grasped and chewed: the forming teeth need to be encouraged and exercised. Gypsies give their teething children a piece of the tough marshmallow root to chew, or a small piece cut from a green willow bough, with the ends made blunt: green willow is supple and does not splinter. Another recommended root is licorice, and this makes excellent chewing. Spanish licorice 'juice' in black, solid pieces can be given, but it does make rather a glutinous mess and the vigorous chewer might well take in a purgative dose. However, licorice can dull the pain and irritation which teething causes. When soreness is causing wakefulness the gums can be rubbed with thick honey to which a pinch of salt has been added, or with honey mixed into a paste with oil of chamomile (prepared like the other herbal oils previously described, only using flowers of chamomile instead of the other aromatic herbs).

The use of a rubber pacifier is unclean, ugly and really an offence against the dignity of the child, and is never permitted in nature rearing. The baby may derive some comfort from sucking at its thumb or fingers or a piece of cloth. When the mouth and teeth are normally healthy and strong, malformation cannot possibly result from this childish habit, though manufacturers and sellers of the profitable rubber pacifier stress the harm of finger-sucking. Thumb or finger can be removed from the child's mouth if he keeps it there in sleep, and in later childhood, when he is two or more, the child can be reasoned with by the parents, and it is usual to find that the habit is soon given up altogether.

Breast-feeding, when the mother is normally healthy and strong, is the easiest stage of infant- and child-rearing. This was meant to be: for in the year or so previous to complete weaning the mother can rest and regain her strength for further child-bearing: this is Nature's way.

With every new child the mother has to choose her time for beginning the weaning from her breast milk. There can be no fixed rule for this. The time factor differs with every individual child, and with the mother herself. As I have already written, primitive women will often suckle their children as late as the fourth year of age: one and a half years is more normal. Women often prolong breast-feeding as part of natural birth-control, as conception is less likely when the energy of the woman's body is being utilized for milk production. That is why, with the energy and vital powers being fully used, weaning must begin soon if pregnancy does occur.

As is well known nowadays, there are natural methods of birth-control which are far more acceptable to those who are sensitively attuned to the life forces than the chemical and mechanical means now advocated almost everywhere. I know that my view-point is not a popular one but I maintain that the 'population explosion' theory does not take all the factors into account. There would be more food to feed us in every land if the vast swarming vermin populations which eat up so much of the harvest were decisively destroyed, and if quality foods were more highly prized than swollen crops of third-rate produce. We could have streams and rivers full of fish, as in earlier centuries, if we were not vying one country against another in the building of great hydraulic systems which dam rivers; if we were not polluting all our fresh waters with foul effluents and poisons drained off poison-sprayed fields and orchards. But all this is gradually dawning on mankind, and may we all live long enough to see our priorities put right.

Weaning is a time of delicate mental adjustment for the child, who could easily feel rebuffed and deprived. The new foods should be offered with enthusiasm and love, with care taken to ensure that the child enjoys them.

No child for at least the first year of life should be given foods more complicated of digestion than simple fruit and vegetable juices or nut milks, or supplementary milk from the milch ani-mals. I have known of children getting red meat from as early as six months old. Lambs also will accept red meat if their appetites are so deliberately depraved that they want such an unnatural food. P. B. Shelley wrote about this in his vegetarian paper *A Plea for Divine Living* (the C. W. Daniel Publishing Company, Ashingdon, Rochford, Essex, supply this booklet).

Weaning can be a simple process. At the start, fruit and vegetable juices are fed to the child before the breast is given, thereby taking away some of his hunger as well as the keenness purely for milk. Apple and carrot juice in raw form and specially prepared by the mother are recommended, and these were my choice. Unfortunately so many apples are now poison-sprayed, and therefore care must be taken. I always chose the sourer kinds of large cooking apples or little cheap ones—usually these had not been considered good enough to be protected by poisons. Once I was in a region of Spain where fruit was scarce, so I bought a whole peach tree, heavily laden with fruits. At another time I had old forest apple trees with plenty of juicy apples that had ripened naturally.

This combination of juices and breast-milk sets the feeding pattern for several weeks. Then true weaning will begin, and the mother will cut down her consumption of liquids. She should also take several charcoal tablets before meals and eat plenty of garden mint—also sorrel if it can be obtained. There are several kinds of sorrel and any will serve.

The great reed (*Arundo donax*) is also credited with possessing powers which inhibit secretion of milk. The white inner pith is chewed, about a dessertspoon several times daily. Drinks of common salt in water are also taken by the mother, and a plaster of vinegar in which caraway seeds have been soaked for approximately ten days is applied to the chest and breasts, using a flannel soaked in the lotion, and binding into place at night for seven nights in succession.

Now begin to omit one breast feed every seven days; give the infant cow's or goat's milk, warmed to moderate heat (but never boiled), and fed by cup and teaspoon. If the milk has been pasteurized, then it should be fortified by adding some 'strong water' (a dessertspoon per cup of milk) made from soaked oats. Add also a half-teaspoon of honey.

After three weeks of this slow weaning treatment, it is time for complete weaning. Give some such food as Nature-rearing gruel mentioned in the previous chapter, or something similar of the mother's choice, twice daily, at midday and in the evening, and follow it with some pulped-up raw fruits such as apple, pear, banana or peeled grapes (if the grapes are not peeled for the infant they are apt to pass through the body undigested).

Frequent drinks of water (or herbal teas), as advised for the breast-fed infant, should not be forgotten. On waking let the child have a drink of lemon juice (fresh lemon), a teaspoon of juice to a small cup of water or barley water, with a half-teaspoon of pure honey added. Or apple juice can be given instead of lemon. By the age of eighteen months or so the child is completely weaned from the mother's breast-milk, and therefore attention must be given to ensuring that the child continues to get a fully-balanced diet, with the same vital food ingredients which formerly were being obtained through the mother's milk.

Now is the time to plead for a vegetarian diet for children. The human child is a natural vegetarian. Place before any un-spoiled child a plate of cooked meat and another plate filled with fresh fruits, fresh salad items and white cheese, and watch from which plate the child will choose to eat every time. I cannot give here all my views on the subject of vegetarianism. It is enough, I suppose, to say here that blood is an ugly food to offer to a child (or equally to an adult). And it should be noted that man, when he does eat meat, always chooses the flesh of the clean vegetable-eating creatures, and avoids the carnivores as unclean: yet man himself is eating as a carnivore! Indeed there is no need to eat corpses when the world is filled with delicious fruit and vegetable foods, and with the milk products which the milch animals yield to man who has domesticated them. I do not understand how man can enjoy these milk products and then so ungratefully seek the life also of the animals who gave their milk. This is one reason why the Jews are not allowed both milk and meat at the same meal: I should prefer them to be like one of the most perfect and enlightened of their sects, the Essenes (who were contemporary with Christ), and not eat meat at all.

That great religious book, the *Bhagavad-Gita* of the Vedic sages of the East, teaches that the ideal food is that which 'increases the sense of endearment' to all creatures; cruelty or killing for obtaining food can never increase the sense of endearment. Food must not be 'productive of sorrow, grief or disease' to any living being.

It is known that Buddha had such sympathy for all living things that during the rainy season he greatly curtailed his travels (he was a wandering preacher), as he did not like to crush underfoot the teeming insect life. We can learn compassion from him: and yet the perceptive reader will at this point glance back to my observation on the need to destroy the vermin devouring our crops. He will also know, if he has read my writings on the rearing of dogs, that I advocate meat for them. Finally, we all realize that very few animals die a natural death—that one animal maintains its health and strength by eating the carcase of another. All the relevant arguments have been published elsewhere, and the conclusion is that Nature meant some creatures to be carnivorous. It is also natural that a certain proportion of every harvest should go to feed wild creatures, and that a certain proportion of these creatures should be destroyed by predators—and so it goes on. So long as a natural balance is maintained, there is no need for man to engineer wholesale destruction—it is only when things get out of hand, through our mismanagement, that we must have recourse to offensive solutions.

The only drawback to a vegetarian diet is that because vegetarians·are still in a minority (although their numbers increase vastly every year, perhaps as a reaction to the mass scientific killings of man and animals) there is a tendency for them to become food fanatics, as if to justify their diet in the eyes of the majority who do not eat as they do! Vegetarians should take heart from the fact that it is their influence that has put vegetables and fruits back on the modern table, formerly overloaded with meat dishes and puddings!

It is often thought that a vegetarian diet is time-consuming and complicated—and fattening. It can be so, but there is no need for this. We can eat our fruits and vegetables—cleaned, of course—as Nature grew them; milk products are even less trouble, for the animal has already done the 'conversion' for us. Simplicity should be the aim—many vegetarian-cooked dishes are quite unnecessarily complicated, even ruined by the application of too much heat to the fresh foods. It was a basic dietary rule of the

Essenes not to mix too many items at one meal—another was to take foods in their raw state whenever possible.

It was from an old manuscript believed to be of Essenic origin (found in the Vatican Library by Professor Edmond Szekely, and translated by him), that I learnt the rule on which I based the feeding of my children and animals; and that rule was not to kill the life in foods by heating them over a fire. The manuscript said: 'No man can sow his fields with cooked or frozen grains and expect to reap a harvest of wheat.' The wheat would not grow! its life would have been destroyed in the cooking-pot! And likewise all foods heated above natural sun heat have lost most of their vitality and life, and when eaten by man or other creatures lower the vitality of the body which feeds upon such denatured foods.

Drinking with meals is another bad practice; the liquid dilutes the digestive juices. It is best to begin a meal, rather than end it, with fresh raw fruit (or vegetable) and then there is no feeling of thirst. Heavily spiced foods, and canned foods with a high salt content, create an unnatural thirst, so that most home and restaurant tables carry a full water-jug as a matter of need.

Cooked foods make for lazy feeding and over-eating. However, as the modern diet of the human race is largely cooked and one does not want to isolate one's children as diet fanatics, one has to give in to their demand for some cooked foods (the sort of foods they will get at the school tuck-shop, at friends' houses, at boarding school and the university, and in the army). Only, for the sake of the gentle and beautiful animal kingdom, at least one can ask one's children to think very carefully before adopting a mixed diet. My own children have chosen to remain vegetarians, although their contacts have made them more tolerant than I am of cooked and involved dishes.

As water is of such great importance to man, animal, plant, tree, indeed to every living thing, it should be said that the mother must do her best to insist on an abundant supply of pure water. I have taken great trouble to keep chlorinated water away from my children, knowing well the lethal effect of chlorine on living tissue. I have tried to live near springs of water, and as I write this book in Galilee I have springs of water almost at my door, and we drink no other water except when on holiday far from the springs. The Gypsies place great value on natural springs, and wherever they travel they know every spring in the area. On my own far travels I have so often gone to the Gypsies to learn from them where I could get spring water. During my time in Galilee, town 'development' has blocked up a wonderful fast-flowing spring in the Tiberias area, when a new road was built. The spring of Abou Essa (Father Isaac), still seeps up through the earth, but man can no longer take the water from it; the only things which benefit from its sweet waters now are the giant reeds which mark where it lies beneath the earth and rock piled up over its source, and the fish in the Sea of Galilee near by, into which it now slowly trickles instead of gushing in a joyous, pouring torrent as it did before man destroyed it.

In selecting vegetarian foods for children, bear these points in mind: Always include roots and leafy things, not merely fruits. (Note also that root crops are less likely to be poison-sprayed than other foods, as it is impossible to spray within the ground—though sometimes they are sprayed after being harvested, to protect them from vermin.) Therefore do not choose washed root vegetables, for it is better to buy earthy ones and wash them yourself—better still to grow your own. A simple vegetable-grater will reduce them to a digestible state for a child not yet strong in tooth and jaw. Prefer local-grown produce, even if less superficially attractive than that from the large commercial market gardens, where healthful properties are less esteemed than large size and a well-washed appearance. Fruits and vegetables lose some of their dietary value when transported for long distances. Greens will stay fresh for a fair period if protected from light by a brown paper bag, while roots and stems are kept standing in a little water.

Children and adults alike could suffer from protein deficiency if the vegetarian diet were exclusively of fruit and vegetables. Protein is found in the whole grains of all cereals, especially in their bran and germ; and in the pulses such as peas and broad beans (which should be eaten raw whenever possible), and in whole milk products and nuts. Try to include some of each of these food groups in the daily diet.

Include also albumen several times a week. If eggs are eaten the albumen is there, but owing to the unhealthy battery system which destroys the good of so many eggs, I prefer to supply albumen for my children in the form of desiccated coconut. Bananas also have properties with effects similar to those of albumen.

Nuts provide not only proteins but also oils, and some oil is needed daily for the human digestion to function well. There is oil in many seeds and of course in the fats of dairy products. Avocado fruits supply an excellent and easily-digested oil, so does sesame seed.

A heavy breakfast is not good for anyone, infant, child or adult. My children never had more than fruits and cereals (and occasionally some soft white cheese) for breakfast. These breakfast fruits included some dried ones, such as prunes, apple-rings, dates and raisins. These dried fruits were never cooked: when not eaten raw they were merely soaked in tepid water overnight, with a little lemon juice added to soften them, and some honey for improved taste.

Further mention should be made of the all-important cereal foods. Bread has for many centuries been the staff of life, and cereals are ideal for man, as they supply the needed minerals as well as proteins, the basic carbohydrates, oil, and the vitality of the sunlight which the cereal grains in their leisurely maturing soak up very abundantly.

Only, sadly, man has allowed commercial interests largely to destroy his former staff of life. Thanks to extraction of the vital parts of the grains for profitable sale to manufacturers of vitamin pills, likewise to removal of the husks (bran) for the same purpose, and to subsequent ensuring of the longest keeping qualities for the lifeless remains of the grains (even if this entails spraying with chemical poisons or additions of equally baneful preservatives, all of which somehow seem to get past the half-closed eyes of supervisors) the product is denatured. The only way to safeguard the wholeness of cereals is to buy one's own grain and grind it at home, or have it ground in one's presence in a local mill, or to purchase health flours from reputable firms who value the health of cereals as much as the consumer values them. The Whole Foods Association of Great Britain and America can supply addresses of such firms and they are also to be found in vegetarian journals.

Unless cereals are fresh and young (and really they should be wild also), man has difficulty in digesting them raw. In former times the conquering Roman soldiers used to descend on the harvest fields when the corn was still young and graze them like cattle. The wild oats, wheat and barley are still palatable when eaten raw from the countryside: Israeli children eat quantities of such grains.

Cultivated grains, through centuries of selective breeding, are much tougher than wild ones, for disease- and insect-resistance, and mostly need some preparation—soaking, grinding or cooking, or one or two of these together. Many peasant communities still prefer roasted, ground grains, pressed into balls with water and oil, to cooked bread. Barley-flour balls were my staple and favourite food in Tunisia. However, I have included methods of cooking cereals in the Recipes section of this book.

As I write this part about the cereals, my son, Rafik, and I have just eaten a meal of fresh corn cobs (or ears), the first gathering from the Indian corn which I plant every year. We ate the corn in its natural form, raw, extracted from the firm green outer leaves and the binding 'silk', improved with a light sprinkle of salt and hot red (chilli) pepper which I also grow.

Rafik remembered a passage in a book which he loves, *Nacar the White Deer*, by Elizabeth Borton de Trevino. He searched out the book and read from it to me, as we ate. The Hermit was speaking:

'Having lit a fire of sticks and dried grasses, and placed on it a clay pot with water into which he had dropped several big ears of corn, he said, "This shall be our supper. Of course our deer shall eat his corn fresh and juicy, just as it comes from the field. I usually do that too, so as not to pamper myself, but tonight the angels will allow us a little feast. And look! I have some salt with dried chilli pods to flavour it, it is so delicious!" '

In primitive times the first cereals which the child took during weaning were premasticated in the mother's mouth, and in that warm, digestible form were spoonfed to the child. The great Arabian writer Avicenna writes: 'After the first two teeth have appeared, the milk diet should be fortified with wheaten bread which the nurse has masticated.' He also advises '. . . and later by bread softened with honey-water'.

Travelling people such as Gypsies and Bedouins, with no time for cooking food, habitually chew cereals, dates and other foods and give the pulp to their young ones who can digest this food without trouble. When wheat, flaked oats and so on have to be cooked, the true vitality is lost.

I remember my friend Margaret Charman of the New Forest telling me that she knew a man who chewed up cereals for his baby son. The boy grew up to become an exceptional athlete and a great horseman. No doubt his father was just as knowledgeable about other aspects of healthful living. When I myself was travelling with the Gypsies I also chewed up plenty of cereals and dried fruits for my children. 'Like the pigeons', friends commented sarcastically, and went and opened cans of prepared, cooked, lifeless commercial baby foods, for their infants!

Personally I see little difference in giving food predigested in the form of milk from the breast or bread from the mouth. Humans eat honey which the bees have predigested.

The legumes are a vital food of man, and it is a pity that they are so often neglected altogether, possibly because they require careful preparing and are more expensive than the cereals. They make a valuable contribution to the health of all creatures, and it should be noted how avid the birds and creatures of the field are to take these crops, helping themselves to peas and beans of many kinds.

The legumes are alkaline (not acid) and are very low in starch, and the human diet is too often over-starchy. They are rich in vitamins and minerals. The life-power contained in beans is shown in the great height and spread that many of them attain (the valuable sunflower likewise shows this tremendous capacity for growth).

All of the legumes when young can be eaten raw and are much more palatable then. When the Gypsies used to hold their famous 'bean-feasts' they mainly ate their beans raw. I remember at Country Garden Shows seeing Gypsies buying up the bean produce from the stalls and crunching them up raw on the spot! When I visited in Spain the internationally famous Gypsy dancer, Lola Medina, she was having a private feast of raw broad beans, and a pile of the emptied pods was on the table in front of her. My children and I share this enjoyment of raw young broad beans and for years I have grown them as a major crop in my garden, followed by lima beans.

I give here an Israeli recipe for chick peas, called 'Fellaffel'; it is one of the 'national' foods of this country. I have not included this in the Recipes chapter, as that is divided into 'unfired' and 'fired' recipes, and this one can be eaten either raw (as I prefer it) or cooked.

Fellaffel

Ingredients: chick peas, matzo flour (Israeli unleavened flat wheaten biscuit crushed into a meal—there are several suppliers in Britain now, but baked flour could be used instead). For two cupfuls each of peas and matzo meal take a large egg, two teaspoons olive oil, one tablespoon flaked oats, several cloves of garlic (raw, finely chopped), salt, red pepper, and sufficient sour (preferably) or fresh milk to mix all to a firm paste.

This is rolled into small balls. These may be eaten raw, lightly boiled, or (as is usual in Israel) tossed in hot oil for a minute. Chopped herbs may be added—parsley, celery leaf, thyme.

Both onions and garlic are excellent eaten raw. To cool down their pungency, pour cold milk over the chopped pieces; or mix with cooked mashed potato or raw grated apple—fine-chopping is best.

From Diet to Sun-bathing

When Alexander the Great invaded Athens, only Diogenes remained in the city and he was taking his sun bath. The great conqueror paused to speak with the wise man, who invited him to stand back a bit—his shadow was spoiling the sun bath. Alexander said later that a great benefit resulting to him from this particular conquest was that he learned from Diogenes all about the advantages of sunbathing.

I have already in this book advised sun and air baths for the infant. They are equally important for the older child. I knew of a man with children at boarding school who used to visit school and take the children away for several days, saying that they had to pay a visit to Doctor Sun. He had them away for nude sunbathing which he considered vital to their health, and the school authorities never learnt who Doctor Sun really was.

It is a pity that nude bodies are considered eccentric or unlawful. Child bodies are almost always beautiful. It is only the unnatural lives which usually follow after childhood that so often turn human bodies into ugly shapes and sizes.

Rain baths also are a pleasure of childhood and are especially wonderful if one lives in a tropical country. We enjoyed unforgettable rain baths in the summer storms of tropical Mexico. Children should learn to take rain on the head and in the eyes, and not to cover themselves against the exhilaration of rain and snow.

Conventionalism in clothing is a health tragedy. Especially deplorable is the modern use of synthetic fabrics which cut off air from the human skin. The modern child is encased in hot, airless, rubberized beachwear! Rubber-soled footwear cuts off contact with earth radiations: all take their toll of human health.

Good food, good water, exposure to the sun; but there are also the questions of suitable exercise and sufficient sleep to consider. Exercise expands the lungs, brightens the eyes, oxygenates the blood, develops and trims the muscles and limbs—it also aids digestion as well as sharpening appetite. Snow, storm and rain need not put a stop to it. Running, walking, climbing, swimming, diving, donkey-riding, should all play a part—and many a boy and girl owes to scouting and guiding the introduction to nature lore which will develop into a lifelong interest.

I believe that there are 'natural' hours for sleeping and waking —but unfortunately life all too often nudges us away from the natural, and we are apt to talk about 'our own natural rhythms of sleeping and waking'. For me the 'natural' time for sleeping is from dusk to dawn, and these hours will differ with the seasons. When I was a child I suffered in the fashion so well described by Robert Louis Stevenson, being put to bed in summer while it was still daylight and having to listen to my companions still playing and calling to one another in the sunlit fields. My bedtime was inexorably fixed at 6 p.m., and how miserable I was until dusk really fell.

Another conviction of mine—and of course it arises from the way of life I chose for myself and my children—is that as soon as a child can walk he should be given miniature tools and taught simple gardening methods. This keeps him interested and occupied, and he can even eat the produce grown by himself. At the early age of four my son was growing plants and shrubs (I remember the exquisite hybrid blooms obtained as seedlings from that wonderful Nature gardener Jean Westlake) and strawberries which far outclassed my own.

Kinship with animals is natural to children; and orphaned birds, fox-cubs, otters, and even young toads, make well-loved pets. The only difficult wild pets are the badgers, because they are nocturnal, and likewise the hedgehog, which has the added problem of being incurably verminous. The hedgehog, lovable as he is (a pet hedgehog of mine in Israel, 'Mateteh' ('Broom') was as clever as a dog) seems to be one of God's very few errors, for neither the animal itself, nor man as a keeper, can free these creatures of the vermin, especially fleas and ticks, which swarm upon it, protected by the closely growing prickles from insecticide treatments. The domestic animals such as dogs, goats, donkeys and ponies, bring health to their owners, as they all need much outdoor exercise which keeps the child-owners outdoors also. Then they also teach obedience to the child-owners: for the children learn from their pet animals how difficult it is for those in command, when simple orders are ignored or deliberately defied!

The child should learn to recognize and gather wild foods, the salad herbs, and the berries and nuts of the hedgerows; the edible fungi—mushrooms and chanterelles. And he should learn to gather firewood and cut turf also for the home fires.

Last, but not least, it is usually the mother's duty to answer a child's questions about the world he lives in, about who made him, about her own beliefs. I think it is generally accepted that if the child is not given any kind of religious instruction he will invent some form of religion for himself; it will be mainly pantheistic and although there will be a strong element of wrath and retribution there will also be a good deal of magic which is full of consolation and promise for the child. The determination not to tread on cracks in the pavement, the determination to go from shop to home in an even number of steps, the determination to keep the fingers crossed until a white dog appears; these are not trivial notions but part of a whole system of prescriptions and tabus which build up into a substitute religion for those who have no other and a supplementary religion for those who have and find it lacking in content. They help the child to fashion for himself the 'strong staff' which religion should provide. Many modern parents are very selfconsciously irreligious yet may themselves have had a grounding to fit them for religious belief. There was more to that grounding than mere indoctrination, and few of them are rebelling against all of it; their children, lacking that grounding, are not even granted by such parents the right to take or leave; the parents are good examples of that authoritarian approach they think they are condemning.

Life is more difficult for the young than it used to be, and I for one would like to think that the blessing of belief is a birthright. Birthrights are abandoned and scorned; well and good, or not so well and not so good; the principal point is that doors should not be closed too peremptorily, by those tall enough to reach the handle, in the faces of those who are not yet tall enough.

Children find great comfort in prayer, and it is a poor-witted parent who cannot explain to young minds why 'answers to prayer' are not always the direct boon asked for. Of course it is not easy. Those who want an easy life do not choose parenthood. It will not be long before the growing boy or girl makes fresh discoveries and initiates new lines of enquiry; at such an age it is, to say the least, an irritating handicap to have no genuine basis for speculation. Total ignorance of New and Old Testaments is not a recommendation in any walk of life.

All children need to have assurance. Fathers and mothers they know to be capable and reliable, but can they cope with the nameless terrors of the night and the roaring of thunder and all the frightening phenomena of the physical world? It is reassuring to learn that there is a greater Power which protects even the smallest child and has mastery over all the threatening presences and hints of presences thronging the world, especially the world of sensitive and lonely children. And, as with so many aspects of child-rearing, it is always possible to combine practice and precept in a commonsensical way. It is sound wisdom to make the child aware of God's love for him, and at the same time to supply a night-light and banish another kind of darkness.

My concern in this book is for the youngest children. These all too soon become schoolchildren and teenagers in a world where living as close as possible to nature becomes difficult if not impossible. They will discover all kinds of synthetic foods which look attractive and please the palate; films and television will try to persuade them that they have been simple-minded, self-denying, deprived and deluded. There will be (earlier than ever today) the inducement to drink, smoke and experiment with drugs, and try every novelty that comes along. However, at the heart of all, for Nature children, there will always remain a core of love for natural life, for the fresh vegetables and fruits and whole-grains, for the sun and the rain, the moon and the wind, and for snow—and for beautiful things in general, because their bodies and minds were formed out of such things when in their mother's womb and in their infancy and childhood.

ROSEMARY (*Rosmarinus officinalis*)

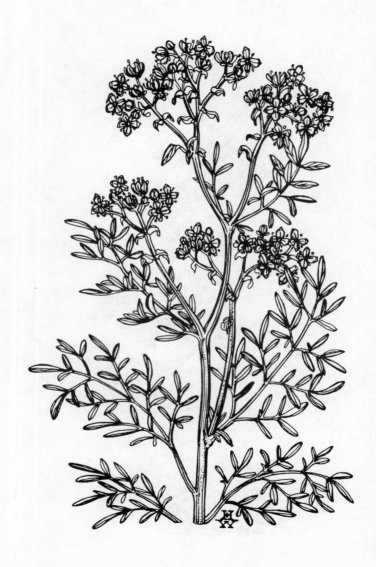

RUE (*Ruta graveolens*)

SAGE (*Salvia officinalis*)

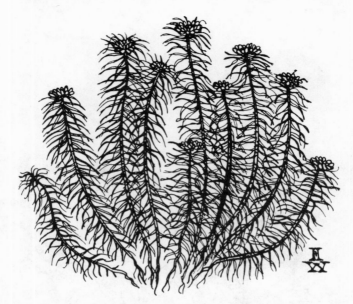

SPHAGNUM MOSS (Genus *Sphagnum*)

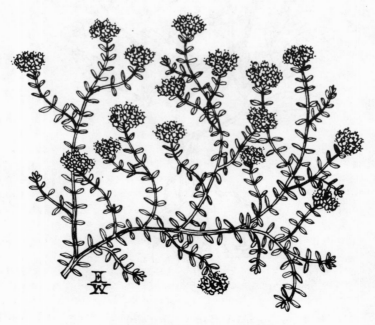

THYME (*Thymus serpyllum*)

6

NATURE MEDICINE
with an appendix on first-aid

❦

I am giving in this book only simple home treatments (on the following pages), which parents can use for their children, and many of which the children can employ themselves. My children, when suffering from such things as cuts, bruises, minor burns or insect stings, know how to treat themselves.

The remedies advised can be found, mostly, in the home or garden. I have left out detailed herbal treatments, as they have already been given in my *Herbal Handbook for Everyone* (Faber and Faber), in more detail than is possible here. There are nearly a hundred and fifty pages dealing with herbal medicine, but even so I am able in this present book to advise the use of different ones, so wide is the choice of natural remedies.

If the threatened horror of atomic warfare should ever fall upon any part of the world (personally I believe that this cannot happen, for the world is not man's alone, it is shared by animal and plant life, and their creator will continue to protect their interests in the face of mankind's increasing selfishness)—then it would be a blessing for families to know how to cure injuries and ills without needing doctors or pharmacies. Neither, in the case of such warfare, might be available, but there might still be good green plants in untouched areas. That is why at the end of this chapter I am including a résumé of a lecture on Herbal First-aid (First-aid from the field) which I was asked to give for the British Royal Air Force, Training Wing, when the authorities were running a course for Army Officers and Senior N.C.O.'s on 'Survival'. As their commander wrote to me: 'How useful

Comfrey or Sphagnum moss could be, for instance, if only a soldier knew of their uses and how to recognize them.'

Medicines from trees are described in my *Herbal Handbook for Farm and Stable* (London, 1951). Although this is a veterinary book the treatments can all be applied for human use, and indeed are often so applied by readers.

I begin with a few general recommendations which need not be repeated:

Herbal Teas

Unless other instructions are given, all are made as follows:

Take one teaspoonful of the herb to every cup of cold water, heat slowly (keeping covered throughout), remove from heat when just below boiling point, then allow to stand and steep.

If sweetening is required use pure honey: there will be no need to repeat the word 'pure' each time honey is advised. Make sure that honey is from bees not ruined by white-sugar feeding, also that the honey has not been harmed by heat treatment often used in order to make pouring into small jars easy, and to liquefy thick honey.

Honey

Honey is good in the treatment of all ailments which afflict the human race, and is especially good in dysentery (although it is mildly laxative it heals and soothes), kidney troubles, heart ailments (it is the supreme non-herbal heart tonic), and in America it is much used as part of the treatment of polio. It is most effective in cases of shock and exhaustion and anaemia in children. It helps bone formation and is useful in malnutrition. However, since honey is a concentrated substance it should not be too lavishly used. It contains up to 80 per cent natural sugar, very different indeed in health-giving properties from the heat-treated cane or beet sugars. Its bee-predigested form makes small demands on the digestive system and it can be assimilated at once by the blood. Diluted in water it will aid all afflicted things. (Poured into the beak of a dying bird it will restore life if anything on earth can do so.)

One pound of honey contains one and a half thousand calories, which is equal to six pints of milk or twelve pounds of apples;

by weight it has three times as much nourishment as meat.

As a bee-keeper of many years' experience, and one more interested in maintaining the health of bees than in taking their honey, I have realized how great is the difference between 'Nature' bees and their honey and bees (and their honey) of commercial apiaries. I grow medicinal herbs especially for my bees, and how well they understand the use of them (bees are indeed great herbalists). They will leave the big scented garden roses for a feast on bitter rue or yet more bitter wormwood, any time!

Commercial honey is sugary in the mouth and fails to pass the true honey test I learnt from my father, which is that good honey pricks the throat when being swallowed. Honey which is substandard in taste and quality likewise lacks full medicinal powers.

Standard Brew

Take one large (man-size) handful of dried herbs, slightly more if fresh herbs are used, to every two cups of cold water. Prepare as above, though heat for longer period, keeping below boiling point. Then remove from heat and allow to steep for at least two hours before use. Over-night steeping is best. No need to strain, as the herbs settle at the bottom of the container. Keep covered also during the steeping period. The brew is apt to sour after three days, and more quickly during hot weather. Therefore, when steeping, use a paper or cloth cover, so as to allow some ventilation.

Cleansing Diet

Fruit breakfast (raw), especially citrus fruits, berries and apple. Some flaked cereal is permitted, such as flaked raw cereals, oats, barley, maize, etc., or puffed wheat or rice, or crumbled rye biscuits or wheat crackers. Do not add milk. Instead soak in fruit juices or honey water or diluted maple syrup.

Midday: Raw salad, to include plenty of garden or wild greens, such as parsley, mint, turnip tops, chives, watercress, dandelion leaves, dill and grated raw roots, especially carrot, turnip, radish; dressed with watered white cheese, a few teaspoons of desiccated coconut (for albumen) to be included.

Evening: More fruit, including some dried fruits, especially raisins, prunes, apricots, figs: not dates. With a few teaspoons of bran and wheat-germ (equal parts), made palatable with a few teaspoons of a mixture of brown sugar and powdered cinnamon.

Laxative

I always recommend senna pods, the large Alexandrian kind. Senna is condemned for griping, but these pains are only the result of breaking down of faecal adhesions in the bowels, and can be reduced by adding a pinch of powdered ginger to every cupful of senna laxative: ginger is anti-cramping. To every senna pod add a dessertspoon of cold water and soak overnight; give dose the following morning. Two pods are put in soak for an infant's dose, from four to eight for an older child. Add powdered ginger. Never use hot water. An anti-griping treatment, if children complain of pains after dosing with senna, is nasturtium seed ground to a powder, a half-teaspoon dose in a little cold water.

Enemas

In fasting on plain water, herbal teas, fruit juices, etc., if the bowels are not emptied naturally at least once daily, give the senna treatment. But when more rapid evacuation is needed give an enema.

In persisting, dangerously high fever, an enema invariably reduces the temperature. I advise herbal brews in enemas in place of plain water, especially a brew (tepid) of rosemary or wormwood or rue or yarrow. Also helpful is very diluted lemon juice (a small teaspoon to every half pint of water.) Directions for giving enemas are in every book on nursing. Remember to expel the air from the nozzle of the enema before inserting this in the anus. See page 40 for further information.

Personally I think that enemas should be used only in an emergency, especially as all children dislike enemas.

Antibiotics

It is a pity that synthetic preparations soon ousted the former natural moulds. They likewise are an emergency remedy. They bring with them the risk of bad reactions in children, reactions which are often more serious than the ailment for which they are being employed. But in a true health crisis they have their uses, and can prove successful.

Abscess

Treat internally as well as externally. Give a cleansing diet (page 65), and treat the abscess externally with any of the following applications, all used hot. Apply raw tomatoes, heated just before use, but not cooked; or a poultice of hot onions; or smear with hot castor oil; or roast a thick slice of pumpkin, cut off the outer skin, and press gently over the abscess; or crush a quantity of nasturtium seeds and make a poultice of them, placed on flannel wrung out in hot water; or use a poultice of hops.

When the abscess has burst, dress with cooling applications of cucumber juice if available; if not use diluted witch-hazel extract.

Aching (body, ear, head, tooth)

Aches in the body are best treated by warmth from sunlight or open fire, and rubbing with oils from any of the following herbs—arnica, rosemary, eucalyptus (very diluted, a few drops to a cupful of hot water), prepared camphorated oil (from pharmacy). Or make a strong brew from pine needles or pine buds or eucalyptus leaves, and apply hot. Also use hot baths in which pine needles or buds or sprigs of rosemary have been infused by tying in a weighted muslin bag and placing at the bottom of the bath, with boiling water poured over before the regular bath water is run in. Let the child soak his whole body in this. Arrange also for sun baths, and sea baths when possible. (Euripides said that 'the sea cures all the ills of man').

Aching ears, if pain is persistent and really strong, call for a medical diagnosis; ears are a very delicate and sensitive appendage in growing children. Simple infections of the ear should be treated by dropping into both ears (no matter if only one is giving trouble), much-diluted lemon juice. Use a small teaspoon of lemon to a cup of tepid water. Massage the base of the ear, externally, gently, and then dry off with dampened cotton wool. Then apply fire-heated cotton wool externally, wound around tweezers; a little natural lavender water should be sprinkled on

67

the wool. Witch-hazel, in same proportion, can be used when lemon is not available, or a Standard brew of horehound herb.

Headache should be treated internally as well as externally with a cleansing diet (already described). In severe headache give a complete fast for several days, allowing only fruit drinks; give a senna laxative each night, also drinks of strong mint tea, and soak cotton cloths in cold mint tea, with a little vinegar added, and bind over the brow. Give also nerve-soothing drinks of lime-blossom or red clover.

Aching teeth of course need dental treatment. If this is not immediately available, let the child chew several raw cloves, or apply pads of hot cotton wool on which natural lavender water or oil of eucalyptus have been sprinkled. Henbane is another specific for toothache. An ancient treatment was to throw henbane seed on to hot cinders, to catch the smoke in an inverted cup, to put boiling water into the smoking cup. The steam is applied to the aching area. Henbane seeds may also be chewed, but not swallowed.

Acne

Treat internally by cleansing diet, bathe skin with Standard brew of meadowsweet or elder blossom, or bathe with buttermilk. Apply extract of witch-hazel to the spots, or a Standard brew of marigold flowers.

Anaemia

Give a fortifying diet of blood-cooling foods, which should include seaweed (best given in tablet form), molasses, raisins, raw carrot, sunflower seeds, wheat-germ, red clover, burdock, parsley. Give young nettles cooked like spinach, served with flaked cereals and butter.

Do not omit sun and sea baths.

Anal Irritation

Irritation of the anus indicates worms, usually (*see* Worms). Make a strong brew of wormwood herb and apply this to the anus. Or apply the oil treatment as used for insect stings, described later in this chapter.

To soothe the area apply a pulp of dock or elder leaves.

Anger

Anger is not truly an ailment. Indeed fierce anger in children often indicates development of a powerful character in later life. But exhausting anger should be treated by nerve-soothing drinks such as sips of cold water or a tea of poppy flowers or of lime blossom. Licorice can be given to chew, and a few teaspoons of dried milk powder offered. Indeed I know several mothers who call a tin of dried milk powder (preferably dried skimmed milk) 'the rage remedy'. Also helpful are teaspoons of honey—especially honeycomb, and raisins to chew or chips of cinnamon stick. My next statement sounds flippant, but I know it to be valid: take the angry child outdoors into fresh air: if it is raining, all the better.

Do not allow the child to overeat when in an angry state, as this may lead to emotional over-eating in adult life, and this is really as harmful to health of body and mind as alcoholism.

Asthma

Open windows must be provided and no mesh-screening over them. Better to provide warm bed covers and clothing at night, and have the windows open, all the year round.

Avoid an over-starchy diet. Give several cloves of raw garlic daily in the food. Give also thyme, fresh or dried, a half-teaspoon daily. Accustom the child to taking a pleasant herbal tea such as sage, red clover or peppermint, sweetened with honey and several chrysanthemum (small variety) flowers or leaves added to this. Several drops of eucalyptus oil dropped on to a lump of sugar should be swallowed daily. In severe asthma give inhalations of elecampane flowers and/or leaves, or use thuja pine.

Bed-wetting

Before describing remedies I should stress that this trouble needs to be treated in a practical way. In a child with tendency to bed-wetting, curtail intake of liquids before sleep. After 4 p.m. only give fruit as liquid, and nothing further to drink except a small glass of milk with the evening meal. At the end of this meal give several charcoal biscuits or tablets and a handful of raisins, which all help to mop up liquids in children. Also give one dessertspoon of dry bran for the same reason. Allow very little salt in the food.

The two herbal remedies needed are rosemary and celery. The former is made into a strong tea, the latter—all parts from root to seed—given raw in salad or sandwich, twice daily if possible. If the strong taste of rosemary is objectionable, marjoram can be used instead. And for chronic bed-wetting, give as salad or tea the 'silk' from corn cobs (Indian corn), about one dessertspoon of corn-silk daily.

Bites

This matter is fully dealt with in *Herbal Handbook for Everyone*. But as children often get bitten, I will deal here with dog and insect bites (though repeating myself) and for other bites refer readers to the *Herbal Handbook*.

Dog bites often entail shock as well as pain. Therefore treat the child for shock (*see* page 97). For the bite itself cleanse at once in running water. Then apply rue or the insect-repellent oil which contains rue and other poison-reducing herbs. If rue is not available merely bathe in salty water, as much salt as the child can tolerate.

After this first cleansing bind green leaves over the place, such as cabbage, geranium, violet, or a pulp of ivy leaves, and then cover with a cotton bandage. Keep the bandage cold and wet. In between dressings with leaves, bathe with a strong brew of rosemary. Infected bites are dressed with a compress of flowers or leaves (take off all thorns) of the briar rose, an ancient remedy for infected wolf bites on man and domestic animals.

Insect bites need immediate treatment, otherwise the trouble they inflict is trebled. Apply at once a pulp of garlic or onion (raw), or apply cucumber juice, or lemon juice, or a pulp of ivy leaves. A paste of whitewash is also good if applied immediately. Wash off after one hour as it also lightly burns the skin. For further soothing apply insect-repellent oil which is made as follows: the remedy should be kept in stock always.

Insect-repellent oil

Pound into a powder the following dried herbs: rosemary, rue and wormwood. Basil also may be added. Take a cupful of salad oil and one teaspoon vinegar to every two dessertspoons of the powdered herbs. Place in a glass jar in strong sunlight. During sun infusion stand the jar in a container of sand which holds the sun-heat. After five days of sun infusion, during which time the jar should be shaken daily, press the oil out from the herbs and pour into a new glass jar, then add a further (same) quantity of new powdered herbs and throw out the former ones (on to the compost heap, ideally). Repeat this once more, making three in all. The oil is then ready for use, after leaving the third lot of herbs in the sunlight as long as possible, at least two weeks. Keep the jars covered all the time to prevent loss of essential oils. This is a proved excellent remedy for all forms of bites, also for burns, wounds and chilblains. When sunlight is not available, use a warm oven.

Bones (rickety and broken) For rickety, *see* Rickets.

Get professional setting for breakages and fractures. Help the child by treating for shock (*see* page 97) and giving internal help to heal the injury, by feeding as many comfrey leaves as the child will accept (anything up to six medium-size leaves). The leaves should be pounded up and mixed with white cheese or sour milk. The old-fashioned name for comfrey was 'knitbone', and it possesses special bone-repairing powers. Holly leaves (trimmed of the prickles) are another remedy promoting internal healing of bone tissue.*

Bad Breath

The remedy is a Cleansing Diet (*see* page 65). As palliative, give seeds of anise or dill to chew, also raw parsley, mint and grated

* Even modern surgery immobilizes broken limbs in a plaster cast while Nature takes over the healing of the bone. The plaster is of gypsum, called Plaster of Paris, and is one more important medical discovery made by an observant layman. Indeed, much that is good in medicine has come that way, without cruel and amoral experiments on living (non-consenting) laboratory animals. Plaster of Paris was the discovery of a French shepherd. He built himself a fireplace from stones lying around the place where his sheep were grazing. The heat of the fire caused the stones to become powdery (for they were from the vast gypsum beds beyond Paris).

Then rain fell, and it turned the powder into a firm plaster. Henceforth the shepherd used such a plaster for setting the broken limbs of his sheep, and soon others began to use his discovery.

raw carrot. Give drinks of strong peppermint tea, at early morning and before bedtime, or drinks of hot lemon juice with honey. Give daily raw flaked oats with a little bran added.

Bronchitis (*see* Asthma)

Bruises

If the bruise is covered immediately with a banana skin (the soft inner side is placed downwards on the bruise), bound into place with cold wet bandages, discolouration of the skin is greatly reduced and the pain rapidly leaves the site of injury. Also the famed remedy of mallow leaves can be utilized; make a pulp of the leaves and bind it into place with a cold wet cotton bandage.

Burns

Here again natural treatments come into their own. There is really nothing to surpass them for burns.

First comes water. Immerse the burnt place at once deeply in cold water and keep there until pain goes. If the burn occurs outdoors and flowing water is available, make full use of it. For finger burns tell the child to place the finger in the mouth and keep it there (moist in saliva) until all pain goes: or immerse it in a cup of cold milk. Burns and scalds are also treated by covering with a pulp of raw potatoes, or whites of several eggs or the slimy inner substance from the cactus plant, or a pulp of that fleshy plant houseleek (which grows on walls and tiled roofs). Hound's-tongue (the plant named after the healing powers of a dog's tongue) is another excellent burn remedy, so is asparagus (especially wild asparagus) pulped up in its raw state. And, finally, if none of these remedies should be available, most homes possess a pot of honey and a bottle of vinegar; smear the burned or scalded places with honey, and then bind over with cotton cloths soaked in vinegar, excluding all air.

Catarrh

First do not let the child make catarrhal conditions in the body by a clogging, over-starchy diet. Too much milk creates mucus. I always try to give some honey in the milk to the weaned child, to break down mucus. To cure catarrh, give a warm drink of lemon water and honey first thing each morning. Serve a fruit breakfast only, and drinks of sage tea. Herbs to use are garlic, especially wild garlic, narrow and broad leaf varieties, wild and cultivated mustard, marjoram, hyssop. Also useful is a tea made from linseed.

Chickenpox (*see* Fevers)

Chilblains

A clogging diet and tight shoes, also lack of active exercise in the winter months, are root causes of chilblains. (I remember an outbreak of unrest among Hungarian Gypsies in a refugee camp in England. I was asked to investigate, and found chilblains prevalent. The Gypsies wanted brown bread instead of white and complained that they could not wear the tight footwear issued to them, so accustomed were they to their high-to-the-knee boots of soft orange or red leather. When their wants were satisfied they filled the camp with splendid violin music—up to that time no one had known that there was a single violin among them!

More everyday remedies for chilblains are blood tonics such as carrot seed, linseed, molasses, burdock. And externally a salve made from primrose leaves beaten into melted lanoline, or crushed snowdrop bulbs applied, or application of the mixture of herbal oils described for treatment of insect bites.

Colds

Treat in the same way as Catarrh. Also helpful are hot baths in which pine needles are infused. A bad congested cold should have treatment as for asthma. A medical brew of rosemary tops steeped in hot cider should be taken at the rate of two table-spoons at morning, midday and evening. Equally useful is a syrup of pine tree buds boiled in equal quantities of honey and water (a handful of buds to a pint of honey-water liquid).

Constipation

Prevention is easier than cure, but where a nature diet has been faithfully followed for some time it is not likely to cause any worry. But with children new to the diet daily roughage from whole-grain cereals, leafy greens eaten raw, and fruits eaten with their skins (and in the case of apples and pears, with their cores and seeds, and grapes with part of their seeds) are all essential to keep the bowels working normally.

Figs, raisins, sesame seed products, desiccated coconut, are all tonic and mildly laxative. To cleanse the clogged bowels and improve their function give a fairly long course (several weeks) of senna pods (*see* Senna, at beginning of this chapter); senna is not habit-forming. Avoid all paraffin laxative products; they leave the intestinal tract dirty and could affect other organs. Much active exercise, with horse-riding and swimming (especially in the sea) are all helpful in curing constipation.

Convulsions

As this ailment is unknown in Nature Rearing, convulsions have not been included in the 'Infants' chapter where they belong. Similar forms of fits, cramps, twitchings used to be treated with the blue or yellow hooded skullcap. A proved remedy and antispasmodic is made from one ounce of skullcap and a quarter ounce each of cardamom seeds and dill seeds and a generous pinch of cayenne pepper, all infused in a pint of sweet red wine. Shake the mixture well twice daily for five days. Then give in a dose of one to two teaspoons three times daily. It must be emphasized that some forms of fit indicate deepseated trouble and are a symptom which calls for expert diagnosis of that trouble.

Cough

First find out the cause of the cough. If the lung area is involved, then put patient on a cleansing diet.

As remedies give blackcurrants, fresh or as a purée. A syrup of blackcurrants can be made by pounding up the berries and then pouring over them a thick liquid made of honey and brown sugar dissolved in hot (not very hot) water, using one cupful of blackcurrants to every three-quarters of a pint of the honey-sugar-water mixture. Give two tablespoons of this every few hours. Also make a strong tea of thyme and sage in equal parts. Spice this tea with a pinch each of powdered ginger, cloves and nutmeg.

When the cough is very heavy and racking, make a tea from the stalks of wild cherry fruits or the bark stripped from branches of that tree. As this wild cherry remedy is very well known to herbalists, the stalks and bark can often be obtained from herbalist firms. Finally a cough syrup can also be made from the flowers of coltsfoot. This herb flowers conveniently in the early spring, one of the first herbs to flower, and it is then that coughs are most prevalent! Make a standard tea of the flowers and sweeten with honey. Give many times during the day. The coughing child can also be given pieces of licorice and pieces of candied ginger to chew.

Whooping form of cough (see page 78). Treat as for fevers. Further to that, the specific remedy for whooping is the small, insectivorous plant sundew. It grows in marshy places in many parts of the world, and is used in orthodox as well as in herbal medicine as a specific for spasm conditions. A tablespoon of the herb (less if dried) is pulverized and infused in sweet red wine, and given whenever required to quell the spasms.

Cuts

If possible hold the cut place under running water for as long as is necessary to check the blood flow. Then bathe with an antiseptic brew of rosemary. If the cut is very deep it may be necessary to plug with clean (dust-and insect-free) cobwebs, which are not easy to come by, or insert wads of sphagnum moss, or place cotton wads soaked in witch-hazel over the area. Puffball fungi can be applied also as a styptic.

If bandaging is needed, place washed healing-leaves between the cut and the bandage. Such leaves are wild geranium (herb-robert), garden geranium, violet, vine and the cooling water-lily. Remember that sphagnum moss is a wound-absorbent padding. When the cut has closed, healing can be promoted by applying a salve made from herbs beaten into a cold cream or lanoline base. Herbs to use here include daisy flowers and leaves, mignonette, knapweed, elder blossom, plantain leaves, St. John's wort, wormwood.

Digestive Upsets

See Indigestion—the same treatments for infant and child.

Dandruff

In children this is often a cleansing effort of the body. Therefore assist the cleansing by the provision of plenty of raw fruit and a weekly laxative of senna pods. Massage the head nightly with a brew of equal parts of rosemary and sage, or a brew of maidenhair fern. Cleavers, the whole plant, provides another proved remedy, very cooling to the head. Make a Standard brew and apply tepid.

Dreams (*see* Nightmare)

Ear-Ache (*see* Aching)

Eczema

Treat internally as suggested for Dandruff. Make a Standard brew of blackberry leaves and apply. Also useful are elder blossom, marigold flowers, and raw cucumber juice. Gently rub the area with moistened oatmeal bags, made by tying soft oatmeal in muslin bags. Some rose petals, fresh or dried, can be added to the oatmeal with advantage. Sunbathe the area of the trouble. It is not always possible to speed the clearing-up of infantile eczema.

Eye Inflammation

Sore eyes, eyes inflamed after a foreign body has caused irritation, yield remarkably to herbal treatment. A Gypsy remedy from Somerset is to brew six poppy heads in half a pint of water with a pinch of saffron powder, and apply the warm lotion. Another is extremely simple: the patient chews pieces of the ground-ivy plant and applies the warm pulp to the eyes.

Other well-known herbal remedies include raw cucumber juice, a lotion of elder blossoms, or violet flowers, or the whole plants of eyebright or chickweed; or the spikes of golden seal and the leaves and flowers of the mucilaginous mallow.

Bathe the eyes frequently with any of these remedies to cure inflammation or soreness. The best quick remedy for 'foreign body' is to hold the eye under running water, or drop in several teaspoons of fresh milk or buttermilk. The Druse Arabs place a small piece of cloth in the ear opposite to the damaged eye, at bedtime, and this really seems to work very well.

Fainting

Immediately remove footwear and loosen the clothes. Apply lavender water to head and nostrils. Give a shock remedy carefully by mouth, such as rock-rose, the juice pressed from elder leaves or gorse blossoms. The rock-rose or gorse need to be pressed into sweet red wine. Or give drops of the Dr. Bach flower remedy for Shock.

The Dr. Bach remedies are especially good for children, and are of many kinds, taking account of the spirit as well as the body. Dr. Bach remedies are obtainable from Mount Vernon, Sotwell, Wallingford, Berkshire, England.

Do not give solid food for several days after a fainting fit, but keep patient on a diet of milk and fruit juices. Give a senna laxative to remove toxic impurities gently, and once again do not be content to treat fainting as an illness, but recognize it as a symptom and have the cause traced.

Fevers

The treatment of fevers is of great importance, because on this are based all the cures for 'children's ailments', from measles to scarlet-fever. I believe there is much truth in old adages if properly interpreted. One is: 'Feed a cold and starve a fever'. This may be explained in several ways. I see it as meaning that if one gives heavy food during a cold one will soon have to treat for a fever also. And in any case it seems confirmed that the natural treatment for fever is fasting (or 'starving').

Of course! And how well have I seen this proved in animals. The feverish animal hides away in a dark and secluded place and remains without any food until cured. The domestic animal is often fed by force when plagued with a fever, because the owner, in ignorance of Nature's way, believes that if food is not consumed daily, death will result! Thus a simple fever often ends in death or in 'complications' which mean physical deformities such as lameness or blindness which are something like a living death for an animal.

During fever the body has no energy to expend on food

77

digestion; all the powers are required for combating the fever and normalizing the condition which is causing the feverish state—for fever is only a symptom of one ailment or another attacking the body. This cannot be said too often.

Therefore most of the ailments of childhood need the same treatment, a combination of rest, cleansing and the use of natural and vital medicines to assist and strengthen the body during sickness.

Chickenpox, Diphtheria, Measles, Mumps, Scarlet-fever, Whooping-cough

These, and all the other fever ailments of childhood, require similar treatment: the short fast, use of laxatives, and the giving of antiseptic natural aids in the form of well-tried herbs and the juices of fruits and vegetables. Serious throat obstruction must be attended to at once, and medical aid sought.

My children never suffered from any of the common ailments of childhood until they attended school. And school did not come until his tenth year for my son because of our travels. Now suddenly came a time of being crowded into a confined place with many other children, and the place was one where the windows were closed either against the flies in summertime or the 'cold' in wintertime! But when the ailments came I welcomed them, for they gave me a chance to impose the short cleansing fasts which all growing creatures need, whether child or animal, and which children are apt to refuse unless unwell.

Neither of my children had diphtheria nor scarlet-fever, nor typhoid nor whooping-cough, but they did have the other diseases, and were never in need of treatment for longer than a week. A short fast of three days, a few days on a fruit and vegetable juice diet, and then out of bed again. No complications and really improved health!

Growing children must have cleansing periods as their glands and other organs throw off impurities; and since much of the air we now breathe is impure, and we are lucky to get truly pure water, the natural cleansing processes are not allowed to serve us as well as they used to; and if modern vaccines inhibit them, the general health of the body will be vitally impaired.

Therefore be on watch for the first symptoms of fever in growing children, and treat the fever by the same natural law which all creatures instinctively follow if misguided 'helpers' do not thwart the natural desires.

Put the child to bed in a cool and shaded room, for fever is one condition which makes sunlight unwelcome. Take the temperature with a clinical thermometer, and base the treatment on your reading. Very high fever requires a lemon-water diet only. Apply cold cloths to the head, and use mint brew or a sprinkle of lavender water on the head cloths. Sponge the body down night and morning, with cloths also dipped in mint-water or with lavender water added.

Use proved antiseptic herbs such as wormwood, rue, vervain, garlic, wood-sage, all of which are the old 'anti-plague' herbs. I myself use them in the form of a pill which I call Herbal Compound, and which I had made up for my veterinary work. It has, I know, helped animals the world over, including cattle with foot-and-mouth disease, sheep with contagious scour, dogs with distemper. It may seem odd to recommend the same type of pill for one's children, but it is logical enough. And parents can make their own herbal pills. Please remember that most of the strongly-antiseptic herbs—in particular that 'wonder' herb wormwood (John the Baptist used this herb so much in his healing work that he carried it around with him plaited in a girdle around his body, and one 'country' name for this herb is St. John's Girdle), are intensely bitter. Therefore prepare them as follows: pound the herb into a powder or pulp (if the fresh herb is used) make a paste with thick honey, and divide into regular-size pills, of about the size of a common 'aspirin' (which I never use!). Now wrap the pill in a twist of fine tissue paper and have the child swallow this whole. In infants the pill has to be pushed down the throat with a finger, in the same way as pills are given to animals (and even to delicate wild birds. I often dosed my pet owls this way).

Give two antiseptic pills night and morning. Plain wormwood or garlic can be used, or the herbs can be mixed; personally I prefer to use several herbs in the pill.

When the fever lessens, then honey can be added in small amounts, a teaspoon to a glass of lemon water (one tablespoon of lemon juice to a glass of water). Give also drinks of the anti-fever herbs such as chamomile, red clover, rosemary, gypsywort, sage, wood-sage, sorrel, strawberry (leaves), valerian, yarrow. Yarrow is dual-purpose as it promotes sweating, useful in high fever. Make all these as described for Herbal Teas at the beginning of this chapter; give one which is preferred by the patient: all are good, all are well proved.

Another adage is that 'old people and children fast badly'. And this is true. Therefore do not keep a child fasting over-long. As soon as the really high fever has abated, fruit juices can be given, any of the citrus juices. Lemon has been taken from the start, undiluted grapefruit and mandarine juice can now be added, orange juice is the least desirable. In countries where citrus fruits are not available give the juice of any berry; among the best are mulberry, raspberry, strawberry, blackberry, black and red currants, gooseberry. First give these healthful and cooling fruits as drinks, but as soon as the child is feeling better the fruits can be eaten whole. While a purely liquid fast is being followed, then a nightly senna laxative is also required.
A daily tepid bath should now also be taken. This is important.

A child in bed is a bored child. This is the time for the pleasure of new 'picture' books and for story-telling, and the planning of celebration walks and picnics when health is restored.

Headache (*see* Aching)

Head-Lice

These difficult-to-remove parasites of course prefer unclean heads, but will also attack clean heads. Orthodox treatment with paraffin or D.D.T. products is usually extremely prolonged, harms the hair, and often is not successful. Using herbal treatment I have relieved numerous Gypsy and Bedouin children of head-lice. Contrary to what is commonly thought these people are extremely clean. For instance a tribal law of Gypsies is that they must wash their utensils and themselves in running water. Yet often they live far from water, and there are times when head-washing is impossible and infection comes from some stranger child in market-place or bus (in which Gypsies and Bedouins now often have to travel).

First cleanse the head with soap and water. Then use a razor-blade to cut off all the hairs to which the lice have glued their

80

eggs. The eggs can stay inactive for weeks and then hatch out: they must be removed. Then apply the following lotion which will cause the lice to leave the head at once, and they can be caught and destroyed in paraffin; the lotion will also inhibit the hatching of the eggs.

To a bottle of white beer add two dessertspoons of the Insect-repellent oil already described under Bites. Shake up very well and rub the hair and scalp all over with this. Bind the head with a cloth scarf (turban style) and leave on all night. It may be necessary to put a hair-net over the scarf to keep it on during sleep. Next morning wash off the oil. Repeat the treatment the same night, and thereafter nightly for five days. The cure should then be complete. No shaving of the head is necessary, no long-drawn-out treatments spread over several weeks.

Another remedy, from Spain: to a quart of very strong tobacco-dust water add four ounces of turpentine. Yet another: make a lotion from a handful of bruised seeds of custard apple infused in a pint and a half of alcohol for at least three days (preferably in a glass jar standing in sunlight).

Hiccups

Hiccups is not an illness, but a tiresome disorder. Catnip tea helps, or lavender water on sugar lumps which are slowly sucked. A surprising remedy, for it sounds somewhat indigestible, is a mixture (a teaspoonful each) of sugar and desiccated coconut. Prolonged and intractable hiccups could indicate heart trouble.

Measles (*see* pages 77, 78)

Indigestion

With normal diet no child should know the pains of indigestion. When it does occur (sometimes emotional upsets are responsible), then treatment should be dietetic as well as herbal.

Keep the child on a fruit and milk diet for several days, giving also a few slices of toasted wheaten bread, raisins, bananas and apples, especially. Avoid oranges, tomatoes, eggs and all fats. Also useful are drinks of herbal tea made from equal parts of dill seed and peppermint (the whole herb). Drinks of sage tea or thyme tea are very beneficial. The child should swallow several charcoal tablets at night. If the indigestion continues then senna laxative must be given for several days.

Also oak bark can be utilized—a teaspoon of oak bark (powdered) to a cup of cold water, left to boil for five minutes. Give a half cup before every meal. Give the soothing Nature Rearing gruel, previously prescribed for the feeding of infants.

Mumps (*see* page 78)

Further, massage the neck gently with warm vinegar and cayenne pepper (a half-teaspoon of cayenne to a cup of vinegar). If there is no fever give a diet of bananas with a little honey added. The banana skins bound around the neck also give much help. The patient will appreciate fruit jellies: choose the type made from an agar-agar seaweed base, and with honey and fruit juices added as part of the mixing water. Or use an Irish-moss jelly and again add honey and fruit juices. Do not forget the usefulness here of pine-buds syrup.

Nightmare

With children who habitually have bad dreams avoid a heavy meal at night, giving the main meal at midday instead. Bad dreams are often caused by toxins passing through the brain area. Avoid frightening stories and entertainments either by day or night.

Gypsies use sprigs of rosemary against nightmare, Moroccans sprigs of southernwood (their beloved mystic herb 'Sheba'), and I use flowering sprays of sweet basil as well as the gypsy rosemary. Another remedy is a pillow stuffed with sweet mignonette.

Paralysis (Infantile)

A Nature diet gives the best protection and provision of sun and air baths and ample exercise which should include swimming (especially sea swimming whenever possible). For treatment *see* Fevers, but it should be stressed that immediate sweating of the patient should be a precondition of such treatment. No untrained amateur should attempt treatment of acute cases, especially where there are breathing difficulties. My emphasis, as always, is on preparing the body from babyhood onward to resist such disasters. If I had to cope on my own I should use pine needles and Epsom salts for the sweating baths and give the patient yarrow-and-sage tea and, during the recovery period, plenty of seaweed tablets, finely shredded comfrey leaves, and molasses in any form, also new pine kernels.

Pneumonia

Treat as for Fevers. Use the inhalations suggested for Asthma (which see). Use also the grey lichen which grows on oak-trees, and which is commonly called 'Lungs of oak'—a dessert-spoon of this, boiled in one and a half cups of water for approximately a quarter hour. This lotion rubbed vigorously over the area of the lungs gives much relief.

Pepper (Hot) Burns

Children sometimes get hold of cayenne peppers or other burning or blistering plant substances and get this into their eyes or on their lips. Apply raw milk immediately, and the pain will soon be soothed.

Poison

If it is suspected that the child has eaten a household poison, or poisonous wild plant or berry, then induce vomiting by pushing washing soda down the throat in small pieces, about the size of several shelled almonds; then send for the doctor. If the doctor is very distant remember that milk and honey are good neutraliz-ing agents. This does not apply to caustic poisons, and it is essen-tial for parents, especially those living in remote places, to learn all about the treatments for poisons. Corrosive and narcotic poisons call for drastically different treatments and guesswork could be fatal.

Ringworm

This fungoid parasite is cured by sealing it off from all air. To do this, paint over the area with undiluted lemon juice (which forms a glaze) or likewise white of egg or nail-varnish. Renew the treatment every few hours, if possible, until the ringworm is destroyed. Internally, garlic will help.

Rheumatism

Treat as for Infantile Paralysis. Further give quickly-cooked nettles, and much raw parsley and the leaves of celery (raw), also raw carrots. Externally, massage with a lotion made from powdered seaweed infused in vinegar. This lotion is messy but effective.

Rickets

Unknown in Nature Rearing. But for children not so reared, treat as for Infantile Paralysis. Pine kernels are especially important, also comfrey. Iceland moss made up into jellies with milk and fruit juices is strengthening for bones.

Scarlet Fever (*see* pages 77, 78)

Sickness (*see* Vomiting)

Stiff Neck

Give warm drinks of lemon and honey and sage tea. Externally apply a castor oil plaster around the neck, made as follows. Dampen with warm water a length of strong cotton cloth and spread it with castor oil. Place this cloth on an enamel or tin plate in a hot oven. When very hot, but of a heat which can be tolerated, place around the neck and bandage to keep in place. Renew after four hours.

Stye

Firstly follow a blood-cleansing treatment. Then bathe the eyes (both eyes even if only one has the stye) with a brew made from the peel or seeds of quince fruits. Or massage with slices of raw potato, bruised so as to free the cell contents. A warm poultice can also be applied, made from nasturtium seeds spread on flannel, then folded and wrung out in hot water.

Relieve the tension of the skin over the stye by gentle massage with pure almond oil, but do not let oil enter the eye.

Sunburn

This can be dangerous as well as very painful. It can even cause skin cancer. If children sunbathed regularly they would not burn themselves almost every summertime. A good anti-sunburn lotion to apply before sunbathing is one teaspoon of vinegar to a half-cup of thin oil, such as sunflower or corn oil. Damp a piece of cotton wool, wring out most of the moisture, then dip in the oil and rub this evenly over the skin. Remember that water-bathing washes off the sun vitamins from the skin. Therefore take the final sun bath after bathing and before dressing.

To soothe and cure sunburn, do not apply oil. Use milk or butter-milk or a pulp of raw cucumber. Or where sun-blisters have formed apply dock leaves or leaves of the white pond lily, and bind into place with damp cotton cloths. In severe sunburn have the child lie in a cold or tepid water bath until he feels chilled.

Toothache (*see* Aching)

Typhoid (*see* pages 77, 78)

Vomiting

Children vomit easily—it is a good cleansing process. If the child is troubled in any way, withhold food for twenty-four hours but allow drinks of honey-water spiced with cinnamon. If vomiting is severe give herbal teas and a pill of grated gentian root in honey (every few hours). Strong wood-sorrel tea calms the stomach.

Warts

Warts are troublesome in some children. They should be treated internally as well as externally. Internally give plenty of raw carrots and seaweed and onions. Externally apply any of the following well-proved natural remedies. All are to be rubbed on the warts at least three times during the day (including immediately before bedtime):

The inner (rough) sides of the skins of broad bean pods.

The inner side of the peel of pineapple (bound over the warts if possible, as well as rubbed over them).

The white juice from unripe figs or from the stalks of fig leaves.

The yellow juice from the greater celandine (the whole plant).

The greater celandine must be distinguished from the common lesser celandine; they are entirely different plants, from different families.

Whitlow

I have not come across this painful condition in very young people. Treatment should be internal (cleansing) and then the best remedy known to me is to cut a lemon in half and rub plenty of common salt into the juicy fruit of one half. Insert the damaged finger in the salty pulp and keep it there for half-hour periods. In between, massage with warmed castor oil.

Worms

Both diet and medicine are necessary—an almost fat-free régime and with the strict minimum of sugar. Food should consist of things which parasitic worms are known to dislike—garlic, raw onion, sage, mint, thyme, salt and vinegar in small amounts. Herbal Compound pills will prove vermifuge as well as antiseptic and fever-reducing. Wormwood, rue, garlic and vervain are powerful vermifuges, so are raw string beans with the strings left in. Desiccated coconut is useful despite its fat content, so are grated raw turnip and carrot. Treatment must continue for some time.

As medicine, give the Herbal Compound pills first thing in the morning and again at night before sleep. The size of the pills is six grain, and a child needs three of these morning and night during treatment. Also nightly, a short while after the pills, give a senna laxative.

Thread worms are the worst of the worm pests which trouble children and they are far the most common. Fortunately the life of these worms is only around sixteen days, therefore, if reinfection of the child is prevented, the worms will die out, as they must emerge and lay their eggs externally to continue their life cycle.

Therefore keep the child's finger-nails very short, as the worms cause irritation around the anus, causing the child to scratch. The eggs then get into the finger-nails and can reach the child's mouth, and they can also infect other children if foods are shared by hand.

86

Externally harass the worms by inserting peeled cloves of garlic into the child's anus. This must be done when the child is asleep, as the garlic gives a burning sensation which is bad for the worms, but also is disliked by the child. Then finally apply the Insect-repellent lotion (see this under Bites). This oil lotion should be applied nightly all around the anus and in between the legs, areas where the worms lay their eggs when they emerge by night.

Alternative treatments are an ounce of fresh rue or an ounce of dried wormwood, made into a worming draught in a pint of water. To extract the bitterness of these herbs (which is the chief worm expulsion element) boil vigorously for five minutes and then steep overnight. Give in doses of two tablespoons every three hours for several days, keeping the child on a diet of vegetable and fruit juices. But these draughts are painfully bitter and it is difficult to get the child to accept them. A piece of candied ginger can be given each time, as 'reward' for taking.

Operations (Surgical)

The Nature rule should be to resist and avoid surgery whenever possible. Man can never truly imitate the wonder of one single organ of the body. An example is the human eye, with its delicate sight mechanism, and self-cleansing and healing powers. Compare the true human eye to the artificial man-made one; there is no comparison. The true one is a miracle of creation, the other is a cheap copy and worthless for providing sight to a sightless eye. Nevertheless, many a person's sight has been saved by surgery.

Tonsils are part of the delicate construction of the human body and they should be left in place where Nature has formed them. Usually if they give trouble it is when they are disordered and draw attention to this fact and to the fact that the whole normal health of the body is impaired.

Treat the whole body and then the sick organs will become healed along with the body in which they are situated.

It would be foolish to deny that surgical intervention is sometimes necessary. When it is a child who is to have the operation, and if the parent has any say in the matter, he should be on a diet of fruit and vegetable juices immediately before and after, and after the operation should also be treated as for Shock, with rock-rose and honey.

Vaccination

I could write a book about what I feel concerning this un-natural treatment. The only true vaccination against all ailments is good health, and the fever ailments of childhood are only cleansing processes and never do harm if correctly treated. There is no true need to vaccinate against them. Needless to say my children, now aged over seventeen and fifteen, have never had vaccinations of any kind, despite world travel along with me. By obtaining a paper from a qualified doctor, stating that the parents refuse vaccination on health, religious and moral grounds, and that the family is in good normal health, people can enter any country, including those where vaccination is a condition of entry.

Likewise I have protected my Afghan hounds from vaccination. I keep my children and animals protected with herbal pills, and have no need of serum taken from artificially-diseased (and tortured) animals.

FIRST-AID

Of course 'first-aid' is sometimes 'full-aid' when one is a believer in herbal medicine, but (as I pointed out when discussing poisons) it is often necessary to act promptly and supply temporary relief before passing on a patient to the care of others. I have already spoken of my lecture written for the R.A.F.'s training course on Survival, and addressed to officers and senior N.C.O.s. I was unable to return to England to deliver this lecture, so I retained the copyright and now pass on as much of the information contained in it as will be useful to those in charge of young children. Because of the way of life I chose for myself and my son and daughter, there were many peculiar dangers and risks for them in their young days, and because of my determination to live close to nature I knew that only my knowledge of herbal remedies and primitive remedies stood between us and possible serious mishap.

Throughout his existence man has known that the world of

growing things and natural minerals is full—as the Bible promises—of cures for illnesses and injuries. Wild plants, trees, fresh and salt water, clay and chalk, mineral springs—we have only to use our intelligence to realize that we, like wild animals, have a constantly replenished supply of life-saving remedies all round us. Using leaves, barks, flowers and berries, and fire when he had discovered it, using earth and water too, mankind accumulated over the centuries a great body of natural-healing lore; and we today have largely forgotten it.

Man was able to heal such severe injuries as wolf bites, clawings from bears, broken limbs, and deep wounds or bruises from enemy weapons, from iron to stone clubs (for man since his very origin was always quarrelsome and at war). Man healed with the use of natural things, for until recent times there were no pharmacies supplying chemical remedies, sterilized bandages and modern plasters.

There are some basic laws of self-healing and self-recovery, and without some knowledge of them chances of survival are greatly diminished.

Firstly there is faith, one must believe strongly in what one is doing. 'Fast and pray', Christ taught, and He was one of the world's greatest healers. I can promise that all the treatments I mention have been used by mankind successfully, through centuries, and I have personally tested them all. They have been in frequent use in my international veterinary work and for human use also. Furthermore, such treatments have often cured cases considered as hopeless by regular medical standards.

Second, the law of fasting in sickness (or when afraid or angry or in any way very emotionally upset). Fasting means abstaining from all solid food, so as to free the body from the always heavy task of digestion of food. An adult human, in normal health, can live for three weeks—or longer—without food. Young children and old people cannot fast so easily. A human being can even live for several days without water, animals far longer.

There were many cases in World War II, in England, of dogs and cats trapped in bombed buildings emerging, thin but otherwise unharmed, after two weeks *without water* as well as without food. People should fast, taking fluids only, when suffering from high fever, severe wounds, or deep fear—such as one experiences in war (for the sensitive and the clever are often more prone to fear than cruder persons). At such times it is wrong to eat heavily, if at all, for food cannot be properly digested and is bound to become a burden upon the human body instead of a help. All who are familiar with nature know that wild animals when sick or wounded go into quiet retreats and remain there without eating.

I have done three fasts of three weeks, and many shorter ones of from eighteen days to a week. One feels weakness for the first few days, usually up to the third or fourth day, and then one's stored energies are released and strength returns.

All the remarks which follow apply to those who have to shift for themselves and those for whom they are responsible, perhaps far away from all other aid. For ease of reference I am classifying injuries and disorders most likely to occur—and, for purposes of this book, omitting advice which is (I hope) unlikely to be useful to parents. It is true that some children do get hold of guns and attack one another with outlandish weapons, but I cannot hope to include all the exceptional cases. So here is my series of recommendations on first-aid practice based on natural and ancient methods. Some are more practical than others, but all are interesting because we have much evidence to support their validity.

Broken Bones—First-aid Treatment

Binding is required to hold splints in place. This is a great problem in Europe as there are few natural aids available. Flax, etc., used for cord needs lengthy preparation. The only vegetable things I know of are trailing plants such as morning glory (not very common), or sometimes twining stems of honeysuckle or greater bindweed can be used.

I think it is quicker and better to cut strips off clothing (such as shirt ends).

Good padding can be made from fresh sphagnum moss, or wads of the following leaves: cabbage, marshmallow, elder, plantain, geranium, cranesbill, hollyhock. If dried sphagnum is used it should be dampened for padding.

Best material for splints is a supple wood, such as waterside trees provide—willow or alder, pieces being cut from bases of a thick branch. Also elder is good. Old stumps of cabbage or kale plants, the internal substance hollowed out, are much used for broken legs of hill sheep. Human limbs would require several stumps placed around the limb—arm or leg—bound in position with circular binding.

To reduce swelling. First remember that swelling is nature's method of protecting injured areas, so do not be in too great a hurry to reduce this. Therefore, tight splints should never be used, and when possible, at several intervals during the day, bindings holding the splints should be slackened for short periods.

In hot weather cold packs are always helpful in injuries, especially when there is inflammation, but not practical when outdoors in cold weather.

Old sacking often found around farms, cottages, etc., washed clean in a stream if possible, or at least shaken free of dust or earth, makes good pack material, with pith or similar as lining.

Mention should be made of plants which promote internal healing when bones are broken or splintered. Comfrey and holly are the most used and are easily found. An old-fashioned name for comfrey is 'knitbone' (*see* page 71). It is rather rough in the mouth but quite palatable, and people eat it daily in salads as protection against joint ailments such as rheumatism and arthritis. Choose smallish leaves for easier digestion; about one handful should be eaten twice daily for aiding knitting of bones. Holly leaves should be trimmed free of the prickle edges, using a knife. About six leaves should be eaten morning and night. Comfrey grows wild in ditches and damp shady corners of fields.

The Gypsies in their lives of constant travel in primitive wagons, and in their close association with horses, often break limbs from falls when travelling over rough places. They are great believers in speeding up healing by chewing holly and comfrey.

Deep Cuts

I am giving special attention to this because it is one of the most frequent and alarming of accidents.

If possible place the injury in running water, beneath a tap or in a stream or the sea, for five minutes or so. Then apply wet cloths or large-size leaves such as dock, sprinkled with a little witch-hazel.

Witch-hazel is an American 'Red' Indian discovery, not native to Europe. It is the best natural astringent, available in pharmacies everywhere, and should be in the first-aid kit in a plastic bottle. Or as an astringent apply a handful of ivy leaves, crushed into a pulp with a stone previously rubbed clean on the grass.

Dried antiseptic herbs keep away flies as well as healing deep wounds. A small supply in nylon bags could be in the first-aid kit. But the fresh herbs can be pulped with a stone and used. In the Spanish Civil War a standard treatment for wounds was crushed rosemary and salt: a pinch of salt to a tablespoon (approximate measure) of rosemary.

Other common herbs of great merit for treatment of wounds are wormwood, southernwood, yarrow. I use such herbs frequently. To give one example:

After the Six-Day War in Israel, a wounded donkey was brought over from Syria, the injury neglected and so deep that flies had laid eggs within it and the place crawled with maggots. I advised applications of dried powdered rosemary and wormwood. Within a week all maggots had gone and within ten days the wound had healed.

The herb yarrow has the botanical name of *Achillea millefolium*, from the Greek athlete and warrior Achilles, who used yarrow blossoms to cure his own wounds and those of his soldiers. It also promotes sweating in fevers.

I would choose as the most important of the wound herbs, rosemary and wormwood, used combined in equal parts.

Very deep cuts may have to be plugged with cobwebs, taken from as clean as possible a place, preferably from outdoors, moved by winding round a stick. Then outside, if obtainable, apply dried sphagnum moss. If possible sprinkle the moss with a little witch-hazel. Never use dirt-laden webs.

I remember in Mexico being asked to help save some cows suffering from torn udders: they had run up against low-placed barbed wire. I put swabs of cotton wool soaked in witch-hazel into the teats (from which much milk was leaking) and then closed the wounds with cobwebs spread over them. The udders were then bandaged to keep the dressing in place—a very diffi-

cult task! Cure was speedy and complete, and I won the friend-
ship of those Mexicans for ever.

Surface cuts can also be treated by laying pads of fresh green
leaves over them. The wounds heal quickly and there is never
pain nor setback from tearing of scab tissue when dressings are
changed. Leaves useful here are cabbage or kale, lettuce, violet,
geranium, and in the lands where they grow, leaves from vines
and castor-oil shrubs. It is enough to apply a thick wad of leaves
on the injury and then bind a cloth (preferably dampened if
weather is not cold). Change the leaves morning, midday and
night, and each time leave the place to air undressed for five
minutes or so.

In desert places the Arabs cauterize wounds by burning their
edges with a lit cigarette. Or clay or mud can be applied when
fresh leaves are not available. I have cured many wounds on my
children's legs by applying wet clay, smeared over the place.
This keeps out flies and dust, and merely has to be washed off
several times a day and fresh clay applied. Antiseptic clay
powders can be obtained from pharmacies; they are not weighty
and could be included in the first-aid kit. The powdered clay
has to be made into a paste with water.

Gypsies (Bedouin Arabs also) use fresh cow or camel dung
very successfully for treating wounds. This dung is 'drawing' and
antiseptic. I remember some Surrey Gypsies telling me how they
cured a case of pneumonia in a Gypsy child by covering chest
and back with fresh cow dung, after the doctor had said he could
not save the child. They told me an amusing story of how they
had chased cows (not their own) 'far over fields to collect the
dung as it fell warm and fresh from the cows'.

Tourniquets. I know of no natural material for them other
than a tight plait of dampened straw stalks. But I would suggest
use of sphagnum moss and witch-hazel to staunch heavy bleeding. When bleeding ceases, then sprinkle on the dried powdered
herbs already named.

Licking of wounds. This can be done, but the lick of an animal such
as dog or cat is far more antiseptic, as the saliva is furnished
with acids to neutralize the toxic substances in foods. An American friend, Ilka Leftwich of California, told me about her child
who cut her head deeply in a fall. While she was telephoning the

doctor, and during the long interval before his arrival, the family Mexican terrier licked the wound without stopping. By the time the doctor had arrived the bleeding had stopped. The terrier continually licked the wound clean during one week, and recovery was complete. Unexpectedly, the doctor approved of the unusual treatment. Therefore when nothing else is available and the wounds can be reached, they can be licked, but the blood should be spat out.

How to prevent infection from setting in. Eat antiseptic herbs as well as using them externally. All the aromatic herbs such as rosemary, marjoram, mint, parsley, thyme, are edible in small amounts. Make nettle soup when nettles can be obtained and fire is available. Salt is not needed, nettles are naturally salty in taste. The soup can be improved in flavour by adding onions, red pepper, flaked oats, if such additions are obtainable. Make like ordinary soup but simmer only for a short time until the nettles are soft. Cooked nettles, of course, lose their sting, and can be eaten also; they are good eaten with flaked oats and a little butter.

Then, to prevent infection, use the dried herbs sprinkled on— as already described—and if the wound requires covering, then make use of the fresh wound leaves already described.

Feet—To Toughen

To harden feet quite a lengthy period of barefoot-walking is required. The feet then develop protective horny outer-skin. Previous rubbing with a brew of pounded-up ivy leaves soaked in vinegar (warmed) for at least forty-eight hours, helps the toughening process.

Barefoot travel. Barefoot travel, being silent, has often saved the lives of hunted people. But it is difficult for a person not used to barefoot-walking to progress at all far. Barefoot-walking should from an early age be practised; dew-wet grass strengthens the feet, so does salt water.

Jan Yoors in his best-selling book of recent years, in America, called *The Gypsies*, tells how easily the Gypsies travelled among masses of refugees fleeing from the Germans in World War II. Not only were their feet strong but they knew how to live off the land without needing shops.

Leaves inside the boots or socks help to keep the feet cool and less tired, when travelling long distances. The best leaves are traveller's-joy (named after the help that this shrub gives to travellers), cabbage, mallow. Also dusting between the toes with cold cigarette ash, or very finely burnt wood ash, can be helpful. *A dressing for cuts, sores and blisters* is honey. Open sore places should be sprinkled with dried antiseptic herbs such as rosemary, wormwood, southernwood, yarrow.

Diarrhoea

I mention this here because a good first-aid kit will contain useful remedies.

From cold and exposure. Warm the body with honey and beneficial spices such as powdered ginger, cinnamon, nutmeg. Ginger at least should be in the first-aid kit.

From wrong diet. First it should be remembered that diarrhoea is natural in times of fear and stress, it is nature's way of quickly removing the toxic by-products of fear, pain and upset life. Too much attention should not be given to occasional diarrhoea.

To counteract diarrhoea caused by:

(a) *Too quick changeover to a raw vegetable diet.* Loose bowels are also natural on a green diet, as can be seen from cows and horses in the springtime. Such diarrhoea is tiresome but not really harmful unless continuing over many weeks.

Natural foods to counteract this are buds of the hawthorn bushes and wild rose. Wild hawthorn fruits (haws), wild rose fruits (hips), wild sloe (plum) fruits (these are very bitter), wild bilberries (also called whinberries), ripe apples. Raisins absorb waste material, swell up, and pass out through the bowels, when diarrhoea is present (they should be in every first-aid kit). There are also the round fruits from the marshmallow plants, which country children call 'cheeses', from their shape, that of old-fashioned farm cheeses.

(b) *Lack of starch.* As an emergency food flaked oats could be included in the kit. Everyone can digest them without further cooking. They can be pressed down tight into a small space for carrying. It is possible to eat grains fresh from the fields as the Roman soldiers were taught to do. They were even seen to graze the wheat fields like cattle! There are also wild cereals distributed the world over, oats, barley, wheat, rye. They can be eaten raw when fresh green. Otherwise when ripe, golden and sun-hardened, only barley can be eaten raw, after soaking in warm water for forty-eight hours. It is then quite digestible. Berber Arabs travel great distances sustained only by toasted whole-grain flour. The flour has then only to have cold water stirred into it, and is pressed into balls with the hands, and eaten. Salt and oil of course improve its flavour. In Vietnam soldiers carry soup of dried wild vegetables along with them.

(c) *Eating frosted plants.* Never eat frosted foods, better to fast completely. Frosted foods will harm cattle and horses, let alone man with his far weaker stomach.

(d) *Eating too much of anything.* It is a mistake to overeat at any time, and better not to eat anything before midday; the adult body really has not digested completely the previous day's food before midday of the next day. I have made this point already. *Colic pains from diarrhoea.* Ginger, licorice, honey and wild anise seeds (or other seeds from that plant family, such as dill, fennel) could be chewed.

Sickness

Vomiting is often a good thing. I do not know why man is always in such a hurry to check this. Animals deliberately make themselves sick to cleanse themselves internally. However, excessive vomiting is exhausting. There are natural aids to help in over-prolonged vomiting, such as teaspoons of honey with a quarter-teaspoon of grated gentian root or nutmeg or ginger added. The patient should always fast and take a natural laxative such as senna. If cause is shock and fear, fast and take honey and rock-rose, also use elder blossom.

Pain Causing Sleeplessness

Add crushed poppy heads to milk and honey (if milk is available). If not then merely give poppy heads crushed into water. When in Granada, Spain, my daughter aged three months was in great pain and unable to sleep, and the doctor said he could not save her. I searched out poppies, made a syrup with water and honey, and fed this to her every three hours; and I saved her. I was able to find the big white wild poppies, but the common red wild kind also relieve pain.

Shock

For all forms of shock use any of the following nervine plants: gorse blossom, wild rose flowers, rock-rose flowers, the leaves or fruits or elder tree, rosemary, skullcap. The Gypsies believe so strongly in the powers of the elder that they are not supposed to burn it for their fires. After World War II there was a report in the *News Chronicle* of a war-blinded soldier. The doctors could do nothing more for his eyes and he was classified as permanently blind. A travelling Gypsy woman saw him and advised bathing the eyes with a lotion to be made from elder blossom and water. The soldier recovered his sight. He returned to his medical officer and was told impatiently that nothing more could be done for him. The soldier took up a paper on the officer's desk and read it out to him. His form of shock had yielded to the Gypsy remedy. For deep shock use the herbs mentioned above, also take honey, ginger, and try to suck any of the clover blossoms, especially red clover blossom.

A pinch of red (cayenne) pepper, swallowed in a teaspoon of water, has been known even to avert threatened heart attacks.

I always recommend Dr. Bach's, shock remedy made from rock-rose, and it has given excellent results. It is available in bottles.

Pain Generally

Remember pain is nature's way of forcing the body to rest and abstain from food, while the body concentrates its forces on repairing the damaged or ailing tissue or organs. When pain is unbearable (a true emergency), chew anything, roots of pulled grasses, though marshmallow gives the best chewing, as it is a soothing plant. Gypsy babies chew marshmallow roots to help cut their teeth. Chew cloth if there is nothing else, for it is the chewing action that helps.

To deaden pain Gypsy people will cause 'counterpain' to themselves by catching hold of a bunch of stinging nettles with their bare hands or holding tightly to thorny branches. Arab women will gag themselves with lengths of their own hair, caught between their teeth; they do this when childbirth is difficult and they know that their own crying creates fear in themselves.

Other Information
More Wild Edible Foods

All the vetches and their pods, reed pulp (the great reed stalks of milk-thistle—stripped of prickles), thistle heads (like arti-chokes) can be peeled and eaten raw as well as cooked, dan-delion leaves, a good salad herb (and also a proved jaundice and vomiting remedy,) the roots, dried and roasted and pow-dered, provide a readily drinkable coffee, especially if the flavour is improved by mixing in a little true coffee and some dried and roasted chicory roots.

'Johnny Turk' in World War I fought for days with only a meagre ration of dried raisins which he kept inside his army cap!

One of the long-keeping wild foods, which possibly could be imported from the Middle East, is dom berries from the shrub 'Christ-thorn'. This is an ancient 'travel-food' of the wandering Bedouins, and the Israelite warriors used it in the Roman Wars, when they often had to survive for long periods without food, when in hiding or when ambushing the enemy. These berries are from a wild shrub, and they are very light when dried and keep good for years. They have a pleasant taste resembling a mixture of apples and dates. I carried quantities when I was on sea-travels with my children, and natural foods were difficult to get.

Insect Stings

Rub wild garlic root over the place. Or strip open the stems of dandelion and apply. To discourage midges smear the skin with oil into which bitter plants have been crushed, such as rue, wormwood, southernwood.

Dog Bites

Suck out the poison if the place can be reached by the mouth. Then apply a pulp of rue or dog rose (an ancient wolf-bite remedy), or garlic.

Snake Bites

Again try to suck out the poison, spitting this out from the mouth at once. Then apply the same treatments as for dog bite, especially rue, the famed herbal poison antidote. Also fast for several days, using a nightly laxative if one is available.

Professor Szekely observed the behaviour of his cat, Arriman, when bitten by a rattlesnake. He was living in an area of Mexico where the rattlesnake bites are fatal. I once saw a rattlesnake there, devouring a large rabbit to which it had given a deadly bite. The cat Arriman clawed off all proffered human treatment and was seen running away to the river, where he remained for three days, keeping his bitten leg under water, and meanwhile chewing at grass which was continually vomited as a cleansing process. The cat fully recovered.

Prepared Herbs

Those who live in towns and have no land on which to grow herbs, and are far from clean countryside where herbs can be gathered wild, can obtain many of the herbs listed in this book (dried of course) from such well-known herbal suppliers as Mintons, Wessex Herbalists, Curzon Road, Bournemouth, England; The Walpole Dispensaries Ltd. of Southampton, England; and the Indiana Botanic Gardens, Hammond, U.S.A.; Walnut Acres, Penns Creek, Pa., U.S.A. specializing in all sorts of Nature Foods as well as herbs. These firms are all known to me as suppliers of fresh high-quality herbs. Then there are the flower remedies, especially good for children, made by Dr. Bach, Flower Remedies, Mount Vernon, Sotwell, Wallingford, Berkshire, England.

In the wholesale class are two firms also well known to me, Potter's Herbal Supplies Ltd., Wigan, England, and Brome and Schimmer, Leathermarket, London E., England.

Like most herbalists I have a few preparations made to my own formulae and a few Nature foods mentioned in this book, especially the Nature Rearing Food for infants (on which I weaned and raised my own children and animals of all kinds, and even my owls!) and the Mixed Cereals Health Flakes. Wholesome foods of all kinds, including vegetables, fruits and cereals, are obtainale in their shop and by post from Whole-food, 112 Baker Street, London, W.1. Then 'N.R.' Products, Blissford, Fordingbridge, Hampshire, supply other herbal pro-ducts, by post, and a list is available.

Personally I do not like to read books in which the author advertises his own products! If the few products of my own which I recommend in the book could have been obtained else-where I would not have had to list them. They were put on the market as long ago as 1935 and have been in demand ever since, for animals throughout that time, and for children more recently. And I am glad to say that the good results they have given have helped to uphold belief in the beneficial powers of herbal medicine and natural foods.

Letters to the Author

I ask readers not to write me concerning personal health prob-lems. I am constantly travelling and not only do letters often enough fail to reach me, but there is no time for replies even when they do arrive. For that reason I have tried to make this book speak for me, so that there will be no need to write me letters. In addition to my herbal work I have the care of quite a large vineyard and herb garden, and I still have several books (as yet merely a large accumulated collection of notes) waiting for me to find time to write them. None of my days seems to have enough hours in it, and very few of my tasks could be put off for a day or two for the sake of catching up with correspondence.

WORMWOOD (*Artemesia absinthium*)

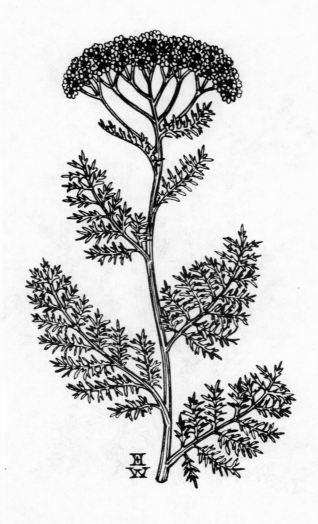

YARROW (*Achillea millefolium*)

7

RECIPES (from many lands)
Most of them 'primitive' and unadapted

꧁꧂

The book-shelves of libraries and private houses are filled with
books of food recipes and there is really no need to add to them
—especially no need as few of the recipes in books seem to be
followed; in most homes the same foods are served day after
day through the years.

Also, who am I to give recipes when I very seldom serve a
meal of cooked food; and further have never possessed, nor
needed, a kitchen in my various homes. I am not a dedicated
cook, but I am interested in food.

The several dozen recipes which I offer now are, I think,
mostly new, collected on my travels and kept because they are
healthful as well as good-tasting; none is complicated, for I have
never had time to waste on elaborate cooking. Most of our meals
have been entirely uncooked (apart from sun-heat), and the
few cooked things mostly have been done Gypsy or Bedouin
style, over wood fires, or very occasionally over a small oil stove.

Throughout this book I have stressed my belief in the health
values of unfired foods, so it would be inconsistent to give many
recipes for cooked ones. Only, as the modern child demands
some cooked foods, and will seek them elsewhere if entirely deprived of such food in the home, I have decided to include such
recipes. The cereals, with the exception of barley and young
corn-cobs, and sun-ripened wild grains eaten fresh from the
fields before they have hardened, have to be cooked for digestion by man. Only it should be remembered that primitive man
of the magnificent bone and the magnificent teeth, as found in

ancient burial places, lived on uncooked foods. There was no sign of cooking on the shards of food utensils found near primitive man.

Quite a number of recipes for sweets are given, as children do demand sweet foods. It seems that all creatures of great energy, such as bees or ants, show this great desire for sweet things, and the human child is no exception. But the sweets that they will buy in shops are mostly made from highly-refined sugar (cheapness and keeping qualities being the prime consideration); and in the refining process the natural calcium content is mostly eliminated. The remaining elements, the carbon, hydrogen and oxygen, forage around in the human system, seeking to rebalance by absorbing the missing calcium, in that way slowly depriving the body cells of this vital element. However, when giving my children the 'fancy' foods I do sympathize with the leader of the Spartan athletes who used to ask people bearing trays of sweetmeats to the conquering athletes to take them away before the Spartans enjoyed them and thus had their appetites for natural foods corrupted!

UNFIRED FOODS

None of these recipes require cooking. Sun-heat is used for a few of them, and several benefit from being chilled. The ice-cream mixes of course have to be refrigerated. It should be remembered that frozen foods are devitalized as surely as in the cooking of them. To ensure cleanliness of raw vegetables it may be necessary to use vinegar or salt.

Children's Salad

Children often have to be tempted to eat up the pungent salad greens, especially the wild ones. The best method is to chop up all the greens fairly small, and that way the semi-bitter things such as dandelion leaves, hare's-lettuce, sorrel, blend in with the milder cultivated greens such as lettuce, kale, broccoli. Include raw green peas and young broad beans (shelled) or raw lentils or chickpeas soaked overnight, all for nitrates.

For 'tempters' add raw grated cheese, small squares of buttered toasted bread, or some potato crisps (packet).

Salad Dressing

This dressing added to the salad does not spoil its keeping properties, as no vinegar is included.

Ingredients: one lemon, half cup milk, two dessertspoons oil (preferably unrefined olive), one dessertspoon sugar, half teaspoon salt, one clove garlic.

First mix the squeezed lemon into the milk to partly curdle it. Then add the other ingredients, mixing all very well together, using a fork; then pour into the dressing-dish the inside of which has previously been well-rubbed with the peeled and opened garlic clove. Note: If a change of flavour is desired, a teaspoon of mustard, or dessertspoon of tomato ketchup or sweet chutney, can be added.

White Cheese Cake (Israel)

Ingredients: one packet or carton of full cream cheese or cottage cheese, half a lemon, half a cup of sugar (has to be white in this case, but use cane sugar), one glass of milk, one packet of wheaten crackers.

Squeeze the lemon, then grate off all the peel, mix this and the sugar into the cheese. Whip the lemon juice into this mixture very well, using a fork.

Now take a long square dish, preferably the kind used in refrigerators, and place a layer of wholewheat crackers at the bottom. On to this spread a thick layer of the cheese mixture, now top with another layer of biscuits, now cover with a further layer of cheese, top this with biscuits and continue until the dish is filled almost to the top.

Make the layers of cheese mixture thick ones. Several packets or cartons of cheese can be added if necessary.

Now pour the milk into the dish. Finally chill before eating, but do not freeze.

Fruit Jelly Drink

Use a packet of powder-jelly for this, preferably one with an agar-agar base. The acid of the fruit dissolves the jelly, no destructive boiling needed.

Ingredients: one packet powder-jelly, one lemon or orange, two dessertspoons honey, half cup raisins, a few candied cherries, the amount of water advised on the packet plus a further glass of water to make the jelly liquid and not 'set'.

Grate the peel off the lemon or orange, squeeze the fruit. Now beat the honey into the jelly powder to make a paste. Beat the fruit juice into the paste and add the grated peel. Now stir in the raisins and cherries. Now add the water, cold or tepid. Shake up very well and place in a cool place. May be drunk after one hour—or any time later—after the mixing.

Dried Fruits Sweetmeat (Tunisia)

Children are apt to refuse cooked or water-soaked dried fruits. The following way of using dried fruits is acceptable to all children.

Ingredients: any sort of dried fruits, especially apricots, prunes, dates, apple-rings, figs. (If the fruits have stones remove them.) To every level cup of fruits add a half cup of coarse sugar, a quarter cup of shelled nuts (any sort excepting brazils, too fatty for this recipe, or peanuts, which are not true nuts). Two dessertspoons candied peel (optional).

Place all the ingredients except the candied peel in a metal or stone pounder. Pound hard for about ten minutes until the fruits are well flattened and the nuts and sugar are reduced to powder. Finally, add the candied peel. Stored in jars like jam; it will keep good for a long time.

Bread Trifle

To use up stale bread; or broken biscuits can also be used.

Ingredients: a half loaf stale bread, one cup sugar, half cup raisins, two dessertspoons honey, two dessertspoons walnut halves, one teaspoon powdered cinnamon, and enough milk to make the trifle really liquid. Some wine can be added if desired.

Remove crust from bread, then cut the bread lengthways and crossways to make small cubes. Pour the milk over this. Now add sugar, the raisins, honey, walnuts, and the cinnamon. (Jellied fruits added to this are enjoyed by young children.)

Peanut Lettuce (U.S.A.)

Ingredients: lettuce (Cos), coarse peanut butter, parsley to gar-nish, and cayenne pepper.

Wash well and dry well a Cos lettuce. Slice it lengthways and spread it thickly with the peanut butter. Chop up finely some parsley, and sprinkle this on to the peanut butter, finally dust over with a pinch of cayenne pepper.

Avocado Cream (Mexico)

Ingredients: ripe avocados, two of medium size, one cup of thick cream, one small lemon, two dessertspoons icing sugar.

Peel the ripe avocados and press them through a fine sieve. Now beat into this the juice of the lemon and all the sugar. When all is well mixed, slowly beat the cream into this. Chill well (but do not freeze).

Flaked Cereals

All children seem to enjoy a mixed cereals flakes instead of the common oat flakes. I have therefore blended with oats, barley, corn and coarse rye meal. And added carrot and parsley, sea salt and herbal spices, with skimmed milk powder, to make a truly wholefood. This is eaten uncooked with milk and salt or sugar. Or they can be lightly toasted in a warm oven with open door, then sprinkled with grated chocolate bar, chopped nuts and raisins and eaten with cold milk. Pine kernels are a nutritional addition.

Also **Flakes Stacks** (a recipe made up and kindly sent me by a follower of Natural Rearing, Mrs. B. Thackeray). Lemon juice and finely grated rind with thin honey, all of sufficient amount to bind the cereal flakes, are mixed with the flakes. These are then made into little haystack shapes of several inches height and left to harden. Or orange juice and rind can sometimes be used instead.

Cream Cheese (France, Provence)

Ingredients: whole cream cheese, one packet or carton. Half pound ripe strawberries, half pound sugar, two ounces candied peel, one lettuce.

Beat all together, the cream cheese, strawberries, sugar, and when fully blended, beat in the candied peel.

Serve on lettuce leaves.

Sweet Cabbage Salad (Roumania)

This is one of the most healthful, cooling and refreshing salads for hot summer weather.

Ingredients: one young cabbage, several cucumbers (enough to make one cup of liquid), two dessertspoons each of sugar, raisins and grated hard white cheese, one dessertspoon dill or anise seeds, salt to taste.

First grate the cabbage on a fine grater. Next grate the cucumbers and strain. Now add all the other ingredients to the cabbage. Lastly pour the cucumber over the mixture. Serve cold.

Raw Legume Salad

Legumes can be enjoyed raw, and that way they supply nitrates and minerals in a wonderful form for health.

Ingredients: one cup each of lentils and chick peas, washed, and soaked overnight in tepid water. Four sweet apples, a half cup of raw pine kernels, two dessertspoons melted honey, garden mint to garnish.

Dry the lentils and chick peas by shaking them in a fine sieve. Now grate the apples and mix with the honey. Blend this mixture with the legumes. Now sprinkle the pine kernels over this, and garnish with the mint finely chopped.

Egg Bread (Based on a Provençal recipe)

This dish offers one of the best ways of eating raw eggs. It is meant for clean, healthful, farm eggs, not the produce from poultry battery houses.

Ingredients: three eggs, marjoram, parsley, watercress, spring onions, salt. Take a semi-stale long loaf, cut off the crust at both ends, then slice the loaf across in two, lengthways. Now fork up the lower half of the loaf, to make it absorbent. Now well whip the raw eggs, and salt them to taste. Chop up the green herbs finely.

Pour the eggs slowly on to the forked-up half of the loaf. Cover with a layer of the green herbs (not forgetting the marjoram, a favourite herb in Provence). Now replace the top half of the loaf and tie it across (cross-ways) with several lengths of tape. Put the tied loaf in a cool place to soak for at least one hour. Finally, remove the tapes and cut across into regular sandwich-size portions. Eat this egg bread with fresh tomatoes and black olives.

Coconut Milk Ice (Tropical Mexico)

Coconuts are a most healthful food. Here is a natural (un-sprayed) food. The milk is not 'pasteurized', the flesh can be enjoyed and digested raw, fresh from the nut.

In Manzanillo (Tropical Mexico) we used to order our nuts fresh from the trees and the owners of the groves would send their men up the palms to bring down the nuts which we pointed out as our choice. Here was Nature food never to be forgotten.

Ingredients: coconuts, one lemon (medium size), three egg whites, icing sugar in the same quantity as the coconut milk, which should fill two tall glasses. Coconut flesh (finely grated) to fill one glass.

Whip the egg whites until stiff, then blend into them the sugar and juice of the lemon. Now add the coconut milk and flesh, mix very well and whip all together until stiff. Then put into ice-cream trays and freeze in refrigerator. Before eating sprinkle with grated vanilla stick.

Uncooked Sweets

(Children can have the interest of making these themselves, without burning themselves, and eat them without (unduly!) harming their health.)

Peanut-Butter Candy

Ingredients: one cup peanut-butter (preferably the coarse-milled kind), one cup thick honey, two cups powdered milk.

Put the honey into a bowl and stir gradually all the peanut-butter into this, and finally mix in the dry milk. Combine and fork all together very well.

Now prepare a shallow tin covered with greased paper. Pour the candy on to this, press down firmly and then cut into squares, or make into circles with the aid of a small, press-on soft-drinks bottle-top. Or the candy can be shaped into a roll of about one inch thickness and chilled hard. Then rolled in more milk powder and cut crossways into pieces.

Apple Sweets

Ingredients: two cooking apples, one cup sugar, one cup powdered milk, one dessertspoon thick honey, one teaspoon rose-water.

Apples should be of a size to absorb all the sugar as they are chopped small and rolled in it. If they do not absorb all (if very big) then add more apple. Now stir in the honey and rose-water. Roll the mixture in a thick coating of sugar and milk powder. Now divide up into small balls or rolls, and give a further coating of sugar-milk powder. If raspberry or pomegranate or bilberry juice is available, can be used as colouring.

Chocolate Balls (or Rolls)

Make as for Apple Sweets, but using two dessertspoons cocoa powder instead of the apples, and blend in a little vegetable fat to bind the mixture and use wine instead of the rose-water. Crushed nuts can be stirred in, also a little candied peel chopped small.

Sesame Balls (or Rolls)

Make as previous recipe, lemon juice replacing rose-water. Use nuts but not peel. Some desiccated coconut can be added. Roll in sesame seeds.

Chocolate Roll

Ingredients: a half-pound slab of bitter chocolate, a dessertspoon thick honey, a half cup each of grated nuts, finely chopped peel with some glacé cherries added.

Grate the chocolate finely and melt it down by standing the chocolate in a container placed in hot water. Now stir in the nuts and peel. Take a thick greaseproof bag, and making a roll of the chocolate mixture place it in the greased paper and tie well at both ends. Chill well and when hard cut across into slices, cutting through the paper.

Blackcurrant Lozenges

Ingredients: one and a half pounds icing sugar, one and a half pounds prepared blackcurrants (such as a good blackcurrant purée, or any good blackcurrant jam), one ounce of tartaric acid, six ounces of powdered gum.

All mixed well, rolled out firmly into a fine sheet, and when dry, dusted over with more sugar, and (using scissors) cut into squares.

Marshmallow Sweets

Ingredients: marshmallow roots, two ounces, fine sugar, fourteen ounces, and sufficient mucilage of tragacanth and orange-flower water to bind. Wash and dry the roots. Then when dried hard enough to powder them, turn into a fine powder. Blend with the sugar and add sufficient mucilage and orange-flower water to make into sweets. Dust over with more sugar.

Peppermint Snow (France)

Ingredients: icing sugar, two ounces, two egg whites, oil of peppermint, thirty drops.

Blend sugar and egg whites and then drop in the peppermint oil. Roll out finely, dust with more sugar, cut into circles using a small soft-drinks bottle-top.

FIRED FOODS

Rice (Basque, Spain)

Ingredients: to every cup of rice add the following: two cups cold water, a small teaspoon salt, one teaspoon each of lemon juice and vinegar (to soften the rice and give a good colour), several garlic cloves, a dessertspoon of pine kernels or hazel or walnuts (or mixed), a tablespoon of butter or salad oil, a sprig of rosemary (one small tomato if desired; improves flavour but decreases keeping time of the rice).

First chop the nuts finely, then peel and finely slice the garlic.

Place the chopped nuts (or the pine kernels, or mixed) with the rosemary (and the crushed tomato if used), all in a strong-based pan, pour the oil or butter over, and soften the ingredients by slow heating in the oil for a few minutes.

Now put the rice into the oil and soften it also, for a few minutes, shaking the pan all the time to prevent burning.

Now add the two cups of cold water mixed with the lemon and vinegar, and reduce the heat to very low. Cover the pan tightly. After ten minutes or so, shake the rice and lift up from the bottom of the pan, but do not stir ('Never stir rice,' they say in Provence).

Replace the lid and heat for a further twenty minutes or so until the rice is cooked. Do not 'peek' (that is, raise the lid) during this further cooking time. When the rice is ready, remove from heat and take off the lid.

If a herbal flavour is desired, then make a hollow in the centre of the rice, and put in a mixture of fresh, green, finely cut marjoram (*the* rice herb), mint, celery leaves, parsley. Replace the pan for a further three minutes.

Try the following additions to rice. If a golden colour is desired, then add a quarter teaspoon of dried saffron powder to the dry rice before placing in the water. Sprinkle the cooked rice with lightly roasted pine kernels (not heated above sun-heat) or some spoonfuls of sweet chutney, or a handful of walnut halves. In Smyrna black grapes are served with the cold rice which is heaped on to fresh vine leaves. In Italy cold rice is often buttered—like bread.

Rice and Lentils Roll

Ingredients: equal quantities of cooked rice and lentils. The lentils should be soaked overnight before cooking. Olive oil, vine leaves (young and tender ones), tomato juice.

Make a paste from the rice blended with the lentils. Flavour with a little olive oil. Now gently boil the vine leaves until they are soft. Fill the leaves with the rice-lentils mixture and make into rolls, each leaf a roll. Tie with cotton in several places across the leaves to hold the contents. Finally, place in tomato juice and heat gently for a further ten minutes.

Celery Stems

Large ones, destringed, raw or lightly boiled, can be used instead of vine leaves,

Steamed Wheat (Arabia)

Prepare like the rice, without the herbs. However, the wheat should have soaked all day in water, preferably in sunlight. Pour out the water, to avoid bitterness. Now add fresh water (as for the steamed rice). Colour with saffron, serve with oil and black olives and cooked sliced eggs heaped on the wheat.

Or, Moroccan style. The cooked wheat can be eaten with milk and sprinkled with sugar mixed with powdered cinnamon.

Corn Meal Mush (Gruel) (Spain)

I ate this healthful food often on the Sierra Nevada mountains of Spanish Andalucia, where it had a delicious smoky taste from the fires of rosemary brushwood and olive roots over which it was cooked.

Ingredients: two cups whole corn meal, also called Indian corn (maize), one cup white flour (to blend it), three cups water, one cup milk (preferably goat's milk for the good taste it gives), one teaspoon salt, two bay leaves (if available).

Mix well the dry corn meal and flour, add the salt. Now slowly stir in the milk. When the milk is all integrated into the meal, slowly add the cold water, stirring carefully to prevent lumpiness. Finally add the bay leaves. Now place over a slow fire and cook gently, stirring frequently to prevent burning. When all the water is absorbed, cover tightly and steam (as advised for the cooking of rice). That is: place the lidded pan in a basin of hot water, and heat slowly for twenty minutes (do not 'peek'). Remove from heat and when cool eat with flaked white cheese (preferably goat's or ewe's milk cheese), sliced raw onions, tomatoes and black olives.

(Very good to eat with this corn dish is the thyme mixture, the Za'arta of the Arabs.)

Za'arta

To every handful of dried powdered thyme add a half cup of roasted sesame seeds and two teaspoons of salt. Mix well.

Za'arta is also eaten on bread, the bread spread with olive oil to hold the herb condiment. Some people prefer the sesame also powdered.

Some Vegetable Dishes

Steamed Onions with Thyme (England: Somerset)

Ingredients: one pound good cooking onions, eight cloves, two dessertspoons sugar, one teaspoon salt, one cup milk, half cup flour, two dessertspoons butter, one teaspoon dried thyme or one dessertspoon finely cut fresh thyme.

Cover the onions with sufficient cold water to prevent burning. Add the sugar, salt and cloves. Cook slowly in a covered pan until soft.

Now make a white thyme sauce, as follows. Heat the butter slowly in a double pan until melted. Now beat the flour into the butter until it is all blended. Then slowly add the milk (warmed), keeping on a low heat until the mixture thickens. Now blend in the thyme.

Pour the sauce over the onions.

This is also the basis for *Parsley* or *Garlic Sauce*. Make the same way, only using chopped raw or boiled garlic, or very finely chopped fresh parsley.

Spinach Omelette (France)

Ingredients: half a stale loaf of bread, two cups of cooked spinach purée (well drained), two large eggs, one medium onion, half a cup of grated cheese.

Soak the bread overnight in cold water. Now beat the eggs well and mix them into the spinach, then mix in half the cheese, and combine this mixture with the bread.

Now grease a shallow, square (if possible), casserole dish, and pour in the mixture. Finally, sprinkle the rest of the cheese on top.

Begin cooking in a slow oven until the omelette begins to rise, then lower the temperature and bake in a slow oven for approximately half an hour. Test for complete cooking by inserting a knife, previously dipped in cold water. The knife should come out clean. Serve cut into squares.

Carrot Flan

Ingredients: two cups finely grated raw carrots, six raw egg yolks, six tablespoons water, half teaspoon salt.

Well beat the egg yolks, water and salt. Next mix the prepared carrot into the egg mixture. Grease a casserole and pour in the mixture. Test for complete cooking with an inserted knife (*see* Spinach Omelette immediately above for cooking directions). Serve cut in long strips.

Peas in Milk (Portugal)

Ingredients: two cups of fresh-gathered, shelled peas to a half cup (small) of fresh milk, salt to taste, and one teaspoon each of chopped parsley and mint, one cup of cream.

Add the shelled peas to the milk which should have been heated previously. Stir well to cover the peas with the milk, add the salt. Place lid on pan and simmer until tender, shaking the pan frequently to prevent burning. This simmering requires approximately seven minutes.

Remove from the heat and add the parsley and mint. Finally, when cold, thicken with the cream beaten in.

Pea and Potato Sandwich Loaf (Spanish Farm: Andalucia, Spain)

This is a loaf filled with layers of cooked ingredients, and taken on their journeys by travellers on the great Sierra Nevada mountain.

Ingredients: a long-shaped wheaten or barley loaf, two large cups each of mashed cooked potatoes, mashed cooked peas, a half-dozen green peppers (split open and grilled on metal grill over open fire or oil stove, or by any other method: the grilling takes about a half-hour), a quarter cup of olive oil, a half cup of black olives, several cloves of garlic (raw).

Prepare the loaf by taking off the crust at both ends. Now slice the loaf lengthways, cutting into four long strips. Spread each strip with the olive oil, making nicks in the bread with a knife to hold the oil. Now spread half of the mashed potato over the bottom layer, and add some garlic to this. Next layer spread with half of the peas, and add olives and the green peppers on top of the peas to hold them. Next repeat the potato-garlic layer, and finally, the fourth layer, again the peas, olives and peppers. Replace the top crust. Now tie the loaf across with several pieces of thin string, and place in oven with very slow heat to lightly toast, or a strong pan upon hot fire-embers can be used. If oven-heated then keep the door slightly open. When the loaf has become lightly toasted, remove from the heat and wrap in a cloth. Cut the strings just before eating the loaf.

Baked Savoury Potatoes (Yorkshire, England)

Ingredients: potatoes, vegetable oil, salt, mustard, cheese, onions, wheaten breadcrumbs. Keep potatoes unpeeled.

Dry well the cleaned potatoes, prick them on both sides, brush lightly with vegetable oil, and bake in oven for about three quarters of an hour until tender. Now split each potato lengthwise and separate. Then add the salt and spread each potato-half with one teaspoon mustard prepared with a little vinegar. On to this pile a fairly thick layer of mixed grated raw onions and yellow cheese (equal parts). Finally, sprinkle with the breadcrumbs. Bake for a further ten minutes.

Nut Roll

Ingredients: any mixed nuts (except peanuts), wheaten breadcrumbs, mixed herbs, fresh or dried, butter, eggs, extract of yeast (such as Yeastrel, Marmite, etc.).

Firstly chop up or mince, finely, the nuts. Now to every pound of nuts take one pound wheaten breadcrumbs, three tablespoons of chopped cooked onion, one dessertspoon mixed savoury herbs such as thyme, marjoram, rosemary, dill—some parsley can also be added with advantage—one teaspoon of yeast extract, two dessertspoons of butter, two eggs, flour and parsley.

Beat the eggs, then mix this into the butter, add the yeast extract to this. Now mix together all the other ingredients, finally blend the egg *et cetera* into this. Pound up well until stiff and bind with a little flour. Roll in flour into a thick roll. Then wrap up in a piece of thin cotton cloth and tie with string at both ends. Now steam in a basin for one hour. When cooked cut up into slices and top with tomatoes and parsley.

Baked Sweet Corn (Mexico)

When the corn is not young enough to eat raw, it can be oven-baked more healthfully than if it were boiled.

Ingredients: as many corn cobs as desired, salt to taste, a little vegetable oil and red pepper (powdered).

Remove the cobs—also called the ears—from the green outer husks, take all the silk off them (this silk should be put on one side to be dried as a remedy for all ailments of the bladder and the kidneys), take out any spotted kernels from the ears, and next lightly brush with oil. Replace the oiled ears in the green husks and place on a wire tray in a moderate oven which should slowly be raised to hot. Turn the ears several times during the baking which should take about forty minutes. Serve salted and very lightly dusted with red pepper.

Sweets, Puddings

Elder Blossom Pudding (English Gypsy, Somerset)

Ingredients: elder flowers, bread, milk, eggs, sugar.

Make a mixture of elder flowers (snipped off the flower clusters), stale bread, sugar, eggs, milk. A handful of flowers to every four thick slices of bread, and an egg to each handful, sugar to taste, and milk sufficient to cook the pudding, which only requires time for the flowers to soften and blend their tangy taste into the bread. The Gypsies often add a few tansy flowers to colour the pudding yellow, but they have a rather bitter taste.

Oat-Tart with Dates

Ingredients: two cups flaked oats, one cup milk, margarine, half cup flour, half cup sugar, one tablespoon sugar or maple syrup.
Ingredients for Filling: one square block of stoned dates, two oranges, one lemon (small).

Grate the peel of one orange and one lemon, and then squeeze out all the juice. Pour the juice over the dates and place all in a pan and heat over low heat for about ten minutes until the dates have softened, now mix the grated peels into this and set aside to cool.

Now make the oat-tart.

Melt gently the margarine, then add the syrup and liquefy this without it coming to the boil. Now mix the dry ingredients; flaked oats, flour, sugar. Finally, add the mixture of margarine and syrup and mix very completely to prevent lumpiness.

Grease a round baking-tin, and cook for about twenty minutes until a light brown colour. When semi-cooked take from oven and press up the sides around the baking-tin, to make a low wall for the date filling. Now heap the filling into the tart and bake for a further ten minutes.

When still warm and soft cut up into triangular portions of typical tart shape. Allow the tart to set before removing the portions from the baking-tin.

Broma (Spanish Colonial)

Ingredients: one cup pure dry cocoa, half cup sugar, and half cup of flour of sago or arrowroot. Mix lightly.

Place in a dry baking-tin in a warm oven with the door partly open, and turn frequently to prevent burning. When all is roasted a light brown it is ready. It is eaten like a cereal, with cold milk. It can be stored in tins and will keep for some time.

Baked Custard (French)

Ingredients: three large eggs, one and a half cups fresh milk, half cup of powdered milk, pinch of salt, quarter teaspoon each of vanilla essence, saffron colouring (powder), nutmeg powder.

Mix the powdered milk, sugar, salt and saffron. Beat the eggs well and then stir them into the dry mixture. Warm the milk to moderate heat and slowly mix this into the rest of the ingredients. Now pour into shallow baking-dish or (preferably) into small greased individual shallow cups (fire-proof). Drop in the vanilla essence now and sprinkle the top (or tops) with a little nutmeg. Bake in a slow oven for approximately twenty-five to thirty minutes.

Red Indian Corn Pudding (U.S.A.)

Ingredients: two and a half cups fresh milk, half cup corn meal, tablespoon vegetable cooking fat, one teaspoon powdered ginger, half cup black molasses or maple syrup, quarter teaspoon salt.

First heat one and a half cups of the milk. Now mix the rest of the cold milk into the corn meal, then combine this with the heated milk.

Cook slowly until it has thickened slightly, then remove from heat, and add, with strenuous stirring, the fat, ginger, molasses or maple syrup, and the salt.

When well blended pour into a fire-proof pot brushed inside with oil, and bake in a slow oven for half an hour.

Baked Bananas (Mexico)

Bananas, when not in attractive condition for eating raw, can be baked lightly.

Ingredients: bananas, oil, sugar, cinnamon, lemon.

Remove the bananas from their skins and place on wire tray in oven, and lightly brush the fruit with oil. Turn several times during cooking which should take about fifteen minutes in a moderate oven. When cooked split down their length and sprinkle with lemon juice, and over this toss a layer of powdered cinnamon blended with fine sugar. In Florida, U.S.A., baked bananas are eaten with jam and cream!

Ice-Cream

The modern child demands quantities of ice-cream. In my childhood it was available only on birthdays, or (strangely enough) as a treat when recovering from sore throats or fevers.

I have allowed my children as much ice-cream as their friends get! Only I made a few rules to compensate me for allowing the excess of ice-cream. I also learnt to make ice-cream at home to ensure that ingredients were as natural as possible.

The rules were to eat some other simple foods before the ice-cream so as not to harm an empty stomach with the shock of the unnaturally cold food. I gave such things as wholewheat crackers, raisins, bananas, before the ice-cream when it came from the shops in towns or villages. At home I made the ice-cream into the basis for a health dish, and added to it such ingredients as dried fruits, desiccated coconut, honey, chopped nuts, puffed wheat, and—when available—that healthful sweetmeat made from sesame seeds, 'Halva', also maple syrup. Or fresh fruit was folded in.

Home-made Cherry Ice-Cream

Ingredients: half pint fresh milk, quarter pint sweet thick cream, three dessertspoons liquid honey, six dessertspoons light brown (or white and brown mixed) sugar, two dessertspoons white maize (corn) flour, one fresh egg yolk, one cup candied cherries. (If available add one dessertspoon of the Natural Rearing Gruel mentioned in the Infant section of this book. It is not essential but it gives improved texture and firmness to the ice-cream and added health values.)

The gruel is mixed with the milk (warmed) and some of the honey, before the cream is added.

Having mixed the milk and cream put aside to stand in an enamel or earthenware container. Then blend the honey into the sugar, and add the cornflour. Finally, pour in the well-beaten egg yolk.

If the milk and cream have been refrigerated warm them to moderate heat before now blending with the sugar, honey, egg, etc., mixture.

Now mix in the cherries which should be chopped small previously.

Beat all together until very well blended and liquefied. Finally, pour into the freezing-trays of a refrigerator and leave to set.

Condensed Milk Fruit Ice-Cream

When fresh milk is not available, canned condensed milk can be used to make a good-tasting ice-cream (and fresh fruit added to replace some of the lost vitamins).

Ingredients: two tins sweet evaporated milk, two teaspoons cold water, two dessertspoons sugar, one half cup fresh fruit such as raspberries, strawberries, blackberries, mashed bananas.

Prepare two tins sweet evaporated milk overnight. (To do this: pierce top of tins and place in a pan of hot water to boil for one hour.)

Then put in refrigerator. The following morning open the tins and empty them into a deep basin. Then stir into this the water and sugar. Whip very well for about ten minutes. Now add the fruit and whip in well for thirty minutes, until the whole mixture turns stiff. Mechanical beaters of course save time.

Pour into ice-cream trays and put in refrigerator.

Sugar Nuts (Israel)

Ingredients: three cups of whole nuts (peanuts can be used when a cheap sweet is required), two cups coarse sugar, one cup fresh milk, a pinch of salt.

Place nuts, sugar, milk and salt in a large frying-pan—a steel or iron pan if possible—and heat slowly, stirring frequently to prevent burning.

(This is a good sweet for the older children to make, as it requires much stirring.) The slow cooking needed takes nearly an hour.

When the sugar thickens to a candy-like consistency, remove from the heat and let it stand for a few minutes. Then stir well so that all the nuts are coated with the sugar. Then turn out (separating the nuts with a fork) on to a buttered board or on to waxed paper. When absolutely cold put in tins and keep them closed.

Note. For extra good taste, though not so healthful, lightly roast the nuts before the sugaring process.

To Roast Nuts. Place in a heavy pan, sprinkle with a little vinegar merely to prevent burning. Cook over a low flame until lightly brown, shaking the pan frequently to turn the nuts. Or they can be roasted in similar way but using an oven with the door slightly open.

Maple Syrup Fudge (**Golden Syrup** can be used)

Ingredients: two cups maple syrup, four tablespoons milk— margarine or nut-butter, an approximate half cup of powdered milk, walnut halves.

Boil the syrup for about eight minutes, cool down a little and add the margarine or nut-butter, stirring until very well blended. Chill. Now work in the powdered milk, using sufficient to make a stiff fudge.

Finally, turn out on to a buttered board and press down firmly. Cut into squares and top each piece with a walnut-half.

Marzipan of Potato Base

Ingredients: potatoes, almond flavouring, nut-butter or milk-margarine, fine sugar, milk powder, almond oil, almond flavouring, cinnamon (powdered).

To every medium-size potato (peeled, steamed and mashed through a sieve), add (while still warm) two tablespoons of nut-butter or milk-margarine, one teaspoon almond flavouring, six drops (pure) almond oil. Mix very well with a fork and chill until this hardens.

Now take one cup fine sugar and a half cup powdered milk. Mix this into the potato, blend and chill again.

Sprinkle with powdered milk and make into rolls. Tie up in waxed paper and use as required, cutting through the paper.

(The 'marzipan' can be given various tints with spinach (green) or blackcurrant purée (purple), or with juice from blueberries (whortleberries) (blue), or raspberries or pomegranates (red), or saffron (yellow).)

Sheets of the different coloured 'marzipan' can be made by the children. Make layers of green, purple, blue, red, yellow, put a drop of water on the top of each layer to hold it to the one above. A five-layered 'rainbow'-coloured sweetmeat can thus be made.

Some Fruit Uses

Homemade fruit wines and liqueurs can be made for health and pleasure. I give a few recipes.

Sweet Red Wine

Ingredients: two pounds of sugar to every seven pounds of grapes.

Into big glass jars (the sort used in sweet shops) put layers of black grapes sprinkled with the sugar. Finally, add a handful of raisins and stir them in. Leave at least a hand width of space at top of jar for the wine to 'fume'. Cover with a tightly tied piece of cotton cloth with elastic band to hold it. Shake the jar occasionally. When the wine ceases to 'work', that is when no more bubbles rise from the grapes, strain into a clean dry jar and cap tightly (the grape residue strained off can be fed to favourite garden plants). Be sure to strain off fruit when it has stopped working, otherwise the wine turns to vinegar.

Fruit Liqueur

Almost all kinds of fruit can be used, grapes, berries of all kinds, plums, pomegranates. Make as for wine, but far sweeter. That is, a thick layer of sugar to every layer of fruit. Add the raisins as advised above and follow all the same instructions.

Currant Jelly

Pick the blackcurrants, or mixed black, white and red, and put the fruit in an earthen pot and stand this in boiling water till the juice flows freely. Now strain the fruit through a sieve without pressing.

Pour the juice into an enamel saucepan and add its equal weight of loaf sugar. Now bring to the boil and simmer well, removing the scum with a spoon as it rises. When the mixture will jelly on the back of a cold spoon it is ready to take off the fire. Pour into dry jars, and when cold seal tightly. (A little of this jelly, mixed with a teaspoon each of honey and lemon juice, dissolved in warm water, is a good drink in colds and fevers.)

Raspberry Syrup

Ingredients: raspberries, sugar, water, citric acid.

Place six pounds of fresh raspberries in a deep glass or china bowl. Dissolve two and a half ounces of citric acid in a quart of water and pour this over the fruit. Then strain, taking care not to bruise the fruit which would loosen the seed. Now to each pint of clear raspberry liquid add one and a half pounds of pounded loaf sugar. Stir the mixture well, using a silver spoon, until all the sugar is dissolved.

Leave open for three days, and then bottle and stopper.

Loganberries, black and redcurrants, can be used in similar way. Such syrups are not for long keeping.

Strawberry Syrup

The same recipe as for raspberry, but reduce the citric acid to two ounces.

Preserving Olives

I decided to preserve my own olives because in modern times

olives are often treated with anti-mould chemicals or boiled to soften them quickly.

Olives are one of the most healthful of foods. The goddess of health, wisdom (and war!), Athene, is supposed to have created the olive to serve as the most perfect of trees. Julius Caesar declared that he owed his health and strength to the oil of olives used inside and on his body. I learnt about olives from Druse Arabs of Galilee. Here the Druse are specialists in the olive, and they farm vast groves of trees.

I choose only to preserve the black olives, as so many green olives are completely unripe fruits, often the olive before it ripens into its natural deep colour. This is, though, a question of variety. The unripeness requires much treatment harmful to the health of the fruit, in order to render it edible. Most black olives can be ready for eating within fourteen days after taking off the tree.

Olives are fully ripe when they begin to fall in quantities from the tree. It is said that the best olives are gathered from the ground: but I prefer to gather them more cleanly direct from the tree into my basket, and leave those on the ground as food for the tree which bore them.

Olives should be picked in a dry condition, not rain-wet. For their preparation for storage in jars or stone crocks, they would first be aired and salted in baskets or wooden boxes (baskets preferably, tightly woven ones to prevent the entry of mice). To top and bottom of basket or box, wire netting of fine mesh should be secured to prevent the entry of vermin.

Into basket or box, layer upon layer of olives are placed, rejecting any blemished ones. Over each layer of olives a thin dusting of coarse salt is put, and several sprigs of leaf (not flowering) rue, the famed olive herb, and when the container is filled to the top, several heavy washed stones are placed upon the top wire-netting cover. These stones help to drive out the small amount of bitterness which still remains in the olives even when fully ripe. The rue acts as a tonic to the consumer of the olives, as well as giving the olives a tangy flavour and acting as a natural preservative.

Every morning shake basket or box well, and transfer the

olives from top to bottom of container, by tossing them up with the hands. Sprinkle over a little more salt each time.

Finally, see that the container, if a basket, has ventilation at the bottom, and space to drip out the moisture; the basket should be hung, and boxes should have stones placed under them to raise from the ground and leave air space between the stones.

After ten days of the salting, airing and flavouring with rue, the olives should be tasted daily. When they are no longer bitter they are ready for eating. They can be eaten direct from the basket, merely rinsing off the salt. But the balance of the crop should be preserved in glass jars or stone crocks. They should not be rinsed for this preserving. Leave the salt adhering and pile the olives into the containers, leaving a half-hand width of air-space between the olives and the top ridge of the container. Now pour over the olives sufficient oil to cover them. It is better not to use pure olive oil, as this turns solid in cold weather and therefore in the winter (when olives are needed most in the diet) it is difficult to get them out of the jar or crock. Mix a thinner oil with the olive oil, two parts of olive oil to one part of thin, using such oils as soya, corn or sunflower.

Finally, the ancient flavourings need to be added: for black olives these are rue, sweet basil, garlic, red peppers and spice cloves.

To every quart jar add several sprigs each of rue and basil, and six unpeeled garlic pieces, nicked across with a knife to let out their pungent scent, and two small peppers (hot variety). When the jars are filled, cover them tightly to keep out air and vermin.

Many people mix water with the oil used to cover the olives. This makes the olives easier to handle, but as this is often a cause of mouldy olives I strictly keep water away from my olive jars and crocks. I do, however, add a dessertspoon of vinegar to every quart jar; it improves the flavour of the oil as well as of the olives.

A final note. For *perfection* the olives can be left in salt in the baskets to mature for several months instead of weeks.

Bread

Seaweed Bread Cobs
Ingredients: three pounds wholewheat flour, one pint water, half

pint milk, one heaped teaspoon yeast extract, a small piece of yeast (about the size to cover quarter of a teaspoon), one heaped teaspoon of sea-salt, two teaspoons of powdered seaweed, one dessertspoon olive oil, one dessertspoon poppy seeds.

Warm the milk and water, add the yeast extract, yeast and salt to this. Slowly work this into the flour previously mixed with the seaweed powder. Now place in a warm place to rise for a quarter of an hour. Knead well, make a hollow in the middle and add most of the oil. Set to rise further for half an hour. Knead well for the last time and divide into small cobs. Brush the top of each cob with what is left of the oil, and sprinkle with poppy seeds.

Bake in a hot oven until browned, just under one hour.

Note. Arabs and Gypsies, fire-baking their bread, make a hard crust. This does not make for such pleasant eating, but it does give increased jaw and teeth exercise, and may well account for the good teeth of these people. To bake a hard crust, use a hotter oven and bake longer.

There is no need to use exclusively wheaten flour in bread-making. The old-fashioned country loaf was frequently made of barley flour; barley was the cereal most used on the island where my son was born. Also a mixed loaf was often baked before wheat dominated the commercial cereal world; the mixed loaf was of wheat, barley and rye, with oat-cake as a very popular food for growing children. All these cereals are recommended in the Bible.

Ways of Using up Stale Bread

There is often stale bread in the house to be used up, and there are ways of making it very palatable. One no-cooking recipe has been given earlier in this chapter.

Panada (Spanish Bread Gruel)

This is favoured by the Spanish Gypsies, only they use raisins in place of the nicer-tasting marmalade.

Ingredients: stale bread, water, sugar, marmalade (orange or lemon), sherry (optional).

Place in a pan slices of stale bread, as much as required, and pour over them rather more cold water than is needed to cover them. Now cook slowly until the bread becomes pulpy. Then strain away any remaining water and beat the bread-water mixture until it has the consistency of gruel. Now sweeten well with the sugar and a generous amount of the marmalade. If liked a little sherry can also be added.

MISCELLANEOUS

A Note on Eggs

When cooked eggs are required, the following method provides healthful cooking. Bring the eggs to boil in cold water. Do not boil for more than five seconds. Remove from the heat and let the eggs stand in the hot water (covered) for five minutes for soft eggs and for twenty minutes for hard eggs.

Cosmetics and Fragrances

Finally, a few recipes for pleasant-scented things to make for the children such as face cream to soothe chapped skin, hair tonic, something for adding to bath water, or putting on pillows and handkerchiefs.

Wild Rose Face Cream

Ingredients: rose-water twelve ounces, white wax four ounces, almond oil sixteen ounces, six drops of spirit of wild roses (*see* page 126 for spirit recipe), some natural rose colouring matter.

Melt the wax and oil together in an earthen vessel in an oven or water bath. When nearly cold stir in the rose-water and the spirit of wild roses and a few drops of the rose colouring matter if a tinted cream is desired.

For treatment of really sore skins, use crushed juice of the wild roof-top- or old wall-plant, house-leek, instead of the rose-water.

Cleansing Cream

Ingredients: three ounces almond oil, one ounce each of lanolin and rose-water, half ounce white wax, ten drops each oil of jasmine and rose geranium.

Melt lanolin and wax in double boiler, beat hard, and slowly add the almond oil, and then equally slowly blend in the rose-water. Remove from the fire and when almost cold add the perfuming oils. As a change, oil of lavender or rosemary can replace jasmine and geranium.

Acid (or Spirit) Perfumes (Lavender, Wild Rose, Rosemary, etc.)

Take any of the above flowers (not mixing them of course), a half pound of flowers to every one pint of best wine vinegar. Place in wide-necked jars, and cover. The jars should stand in a warm place, such as in hot sunlight, or several hours daily by a warm oven. The jars are required to stand for a fortnight. Shake the contents well every day, and every five days press out the flowers, discard them and add fresh ones. When ready strain and filter and bottle, capping well to exclude all air.

Tonic Spirits of Lavender, etc.

Ingredients: two handfuls of dried lavender flowers, half a cup each of mace and nutmeg, one dessertspoon each of cloves and cinnamon, one quart spirits. Alternatively use rosemary, basil, etc.

Pulverize all the ingredients very well and then pour over the mixture the quart of spirits. Let the solution stand in a warm place for two weeks, shake up very well each day. At the end of the two weeks strain and bottle.

(One teaspoon or less, sweetened with honey or sugar, taken in a quarter cup of water several times daily, is good for headache and nervous disorders.)

Queen of Hungary's Lotion (Rosemary and Lavender)

To apply in fevers and headaches or just to soothe the nerves.

Take spirit of rosemary one and a half pints, spirit of lavender half a pint, rose-water four ounces, and mix all together and let them stand in a warm place for several days. Then shake very well for fifteen minutes, and bottle ready for use, capping tightly.

A Powerful Hair Tonic

Burn in an old tin (incinerate), two ounces each of fresh or dried rosemary, southernwood, myrtle berries and hazel bark. Make a strong solution of the ashes by adding to them a pint of hot water (heated rain-water preferably), strain well.

Rub the roots of the hair with this.

An Ancient Way of making Natural Flower Perfumes for use in the Nursery

Take any of these fragrant flowers:

White Jasmine, Violets, Lily-of-the-Valley, Woodruff, Rosemary, Lavender, Clove-Pinks, Wallflowers.

Now fold pieces of white cotton cloth four times and moisten them with pure olive oil, slightly pressing them. Then place the cloths over wooden frames. Next spread in thick layers on the cloths, flowers chosen to be the perfume, such as jasmine, for instance. The flowers can be fresh or dried and should be deprived of all green parts.

After twenty-four hours remove all flowers and replace with fresh ones, continuing until the oil is sufficiently perfumed.

The flowers are then removed finally, and the cloths are gently steamed over moderate heat, and the oil is pressed out into shallow dishes ready for bottling and capping tightly.

'Lavender Blue' Tooth Powder

Ingredients: bicarbonate of soda a half ounce, powdered cuttle-fish bone a half ounce, precipitated chalk six ounces, oil of lavender six ounces, a pinch of washing blue powder.

(The children can find cuttlefish bone along the seashore, where it is frequently to be found washed up with other sea-wrack. This substance is also very good for cage-birds.)

Blend all the dry ingredients, then drop in the lavender oil slowly and mix further.

Note: A good and very natural (charcoal) dentifrice can be made from burnt bread as follows. Burn some bread crusts and crush to a fine powder, and mix with half their quantity of icing sugar and talcum powder. Flavour with a few drops of oil of peppermint.

8

CONCLUSION

✃✃✃

I have reached the end of a short book which I planned to write many years ago!

Indeed, each time that I used natural treatments or diets to cure my children or other people's children of injuries or ills (for in this modern world total health is difficult to attain and maintain), I always decided to write such a book with no more delay. For I wished to remind parents of young children that Nature laws still exist, and that the powers of Nature remain as they have been since the creation of the universe, ready to restore to normal the abnormal; and the abnormal for the human body is sickness, no matter what form it takes.

In technical books it is quite general to quote from authorities who are likely to impress the readers with their findings more than the author writing the book can expect to impress, and therefore I shall likewise quote a little from the great in medicine whose names are known where mine is unknown!

Hippocrates is strangely upheld as being the father of all medicine (including modern medicine), though his simple basic treatments for all kinds of human ailments (oxymel, a mixture of vinegar and honey, and hydromel, a mixture of honey and water) would seem out-of-place in modern scientific and chemical-ridden medicine. He wrote:

'In my opinion every doctor must have a knowledge of Nature, and, if he is to do his duty, make every effort to learn the relation of the human organism to articles of food and drink, and to every kind of habit, and the effects produced on each individual by each.'

It was also Hippocrates who uttered the edict which should

really stand behind all medical practice: 'Let food be your medicine, and let medicine be your food.'

However, it is difficult to commercialize such simple teachings (and medicine supports vast commercial interests), therefore a new medical 'God' was chosen, a chemist not a doctor: Louis Pasteur. It was Pasteur who to my mind brought ugliness and darkness into medicine, popularizing medical experiments on animals and advocating vaccination.

Because of my sympathy for laboratory animals (their sufferings are daily in my thoughts) and because of my detestation of the unnatural in any form, in medicine or anything else, I could never respect Pasteur, and chose to follow Hippocrates and many of the great Jewish and Arabian medical teachers, from Avicenna the Arabian to Christ and Maimonides of the Jews. It was Christ who said, 'Fast and pray', and He healed the multitudes, thus laying down precepts of eternal validity.

Moses Maimonides was a spiritual giant of eight centuries ago. He is buried in Tiberias, in Galilee, and I have made many pilgrimages to his tomb. In his later years he was chief physician to the Emperor Saladin at the time when the Saracens were fighting against the Crusaders. This Maimonides was physician, philosopher, author, scientist, astronomer, rabbi, and his teachings are receiving new acclaim today as their wisdom is seen to be untarnished even in our times. All those centuries ago Maimonides stressed the importance of wholewheat flour for the people's bread, and the importance of choosing one's dwelling-place where there were good uncontaminated air and water—as both are the pillars of good health for every living thing, and nothing can supersede them.

We all know the importance of fresh air: thus the importance of country-living. Then since two-thirds of the body is water, the necessity of good water is indisputable. And yet modern mankind consistently accepts both impure air and denatured water.

And well Maimonides understood the true nature of man; that men have a dual nature, and are matter and spirit, body and soul, heaven and earth.

We have to look after the welfare of the child's soul as well as the body. Maimonides said that there were two purposes to the Holy Law, the welfare of the soul and the welfare of the body.

He taught that man should strive for physical health so that his body and limbs would grow as God planned for the perfect form of Man, and therefore his soul could attain moral and intellectual eminence without the hindrance of a sick body.

Being careful about what we parents eat, and give our children to eat, is often described as 'fussy' or 'fanatical' by those who eat mainly what the food advertisements tell them is enjoyable eating. And again, these people living on lifeless commercialized foods, and in addition many of them heavy smokers and lovers of alcohol, point out, truly enough, that they manage to keep healthy and live long. Only the truth is that they are living on the reserves of health bequeathed to them by their ancestors who did live healthily because in former times foods were more natural and complete; slowly those reserves will all be used up and then it will be seen that it is impossible to sustain normal health by an abnormal way of living.

Maimonides, like Hippocrates before him, taught his disciples that man should eat and drink in order to strengthen and heal his body and limbs. '. . . let him select foods that are healthful even if they are not good-tasing always.' So often in my travels with my children, when giving them their daily meals, mostly of raw foods (chosen with much care to avoid chemical-sprayed produce), scoffers have gathered around to warn that my children would starve soon on such 'plain' foods, so unlike 'the proper foods which everyone eats'. The scoffers themselves were all sorts of shapes and sizes, the sorts of shapes that 'proper' foods make of many human beings.

Sometimes we met kindred spirits, mostly the Gypsies or peasant people, who ate rather in the way that we did (we ate many a meal when on foot or on donkey-back, as the travelling Gypsies do.)

But the recipes given in this book show that the children's meals were often interesting and varied, and that I could stretch a point occasionally, knowing that I have built up sound constitutions. After all, food remains one of the simple pleasures of childhood. Over-strictness always causes rebellion and distaste.

I remember once in Paris, when criticism as to the 'poor way' in which I was feeding my children was especially strong, a letter arrived for me from Professor Bordeux Szekely, the Hungarian doctor, author and dietician. The letter is dated as long ago as August 5th 1957, and in it Professor Szekely wrote:

'Your children's diet sounds excellent, and meets with my complete approval.'

I give basically the same meals to my children today. They are both of high-school age now. My son now studies at an Israel Naval College. There is a vegetarian table at the college for those students who wish to eat such foods; therefore he manages very well.

And finally, concerning Maimonides, I think his observation about the Messiah (for whose coming the whole world is waiting) seems especially appropriate for our time. He says that with the coming of the Messiah we need not imagine that the Laws of Nature will disappear or that new creations will emerge. The Laws of Nature are unchanging and man cannot override them. The same Natural Laws are as fixed today as when the universe was created. Only in our own time we suffer from a new condition, a state of world pollution which would have been unthinkable in the era of Maimonides.

Not only is the earth poisoned, but even the sea, that former great healer of the ills of mankind, is showing an alarming saturation of harmful chemicals in many oceans of the world. Farmlands are sprayed with chemicals against pests which attack the crops because in many cases those crops are unnaturally raised; then come the rains which wash vegetation and the land fairly clean, and the rains, now unclean themselves, drain into the rivers. 'All rivers lead to the sea', we read in Ecclesiastes. But instead of the clean, gushing, sparkling waters of former times (and I remember such rivers in my childhood, although there were also some polluted ones to be seen and smelt), we now see rivers frothing with detergents, or streaked with chemicals, or darkened with sewage discharged into them.

As I write these lines, in late June, 1969, information comes over the radio, that the great river Rhine is poisoned where it flows in Holland. Chemical wastes entering the river in Germany are the cause. Vast numbers of fish are already dead. The people are warned not to drink it, nor even to bathe in it, until the waters become safe again. (Only what of the teeming wild animals who also use the Rhine and do not hear radio announcements—they will die!)

It is a sad and true fact that we are raising our children in a difficult time in the life history of Man. Our daily bread is mainly lifeless and chemicalized (unless we bake our own, and then it is difficult for some to get flour which has not been de-natured), and man's eyes and soul (and the children's eyes and souls) are too often fed with ugly literature and equally ugly cinema, theatre and television (because the unbeautiful has been proved commercially profitable). Therefore we must make allowances for our children and accept their new way of life, even though we feel that it differs overmuch from the life which we esteem as sensible and admirable.

Years ago I copied out some lines on the human child, and regret that I never took down also the name of the author (perhaps no author was given). Often when I feel like raging at my children because of their insistence on doing something of which I do not approve, or merely do not want them to do, I keep quiet and read instead the lines: 'If you want to understand a child you must also love him and not condemn him. You must play with him, watch his movements, his idiosyncrasies, his ways of behaviour; but if you merely condemn, resist or blame him, there is no comprehension of the child.'

Nowadays we like to hurry over everything, there seems to be no time left to 'stand and stare'—nor to daydream. Women are impatient about preparing home foods for their children, and seek things prepared in the factory, which merely need to be opened up with a knife or a can-opener. Years ago, for my own good, to combat my own personal laziness in household tasks, I copied out a record of some of the work which was normal to the seventeenth-century English housewife. Here it is:

'She is expected to have skill in hemp and flax from the winding to its pulling, preparing, washing, drying, spinning and reeling. Skill in dyeing of wool from her home dyes including oak galls, madder, puke and the staining berries. Skill in wines, and in the making of beer, ale, perry and cyder. The office of the maltster as this is properly the work of women, for it is housework done altogether within doors, the man only ought to bring in and provide the grain. Skill in the preparing of whey drinks, called whyfe, the best refreshments to quench the thirst of the workers in the harvest fields. Skill in dairying, milking, preparing of creams and cheeses, butter-making and powdering and potting of same. Skill in baking the home loaf of wheat, barley and rye, and the preparing of oatmeal which is the crown of the housewife's garland. The conserving of the garden and orchard fruits into syrups, jams and jellies. The drying and preparing of herbs for medicine and for pleasure in sachets and pot-pourris.'

And what of modern man? The following is a true estimation: 'In a materialistic world, where time is reckoned as money and the dignity of honest work is degraded into terms of "man-hours", this precious thing "time" is begrudged its gentle influence. Man is unwilling to "wait upon the Lord" either in his heart or in his daily activities. He seeks a short cut to maturity and likes to deceive himself and the public that his products attain the same quality, because they appear so to the eye.' The example of wheat is then given. How, 'when wheat is cut for the harvesting there is always a certain amount of moisture in the berry, no matter how good the season has been. When the corn has stood in the stack for some months this moisture will have undergone natural evaporation and there will then be perfect grain for the milling, provided the stacks have been cared for properly. However, the moisture in the wheat berries can be extracted by man within a few hours if he chooses, merely by putting the corn into a drying plant. On analysis the berries will be found to be as dry if not drier than when matured slowly in the stack. But the quality is not the same, and every old miller with a lifetime's experience in handling grain, knows very well that it is not the same. Nor will bread made from the quickly-dried wheat have the same health value as when made from wheat slowly matured. Indeed life itself cannot be subjected to analysis, because it is invisible. It cannot be proved. It can only be sensed. There is no difference in *analysis* between a wheat berry that has been "killed" in a drying machine and one that has been allowed to grow mellow with age in the stack.'

I remember a Danish cheesemaker telling me that groups came from abroad to pay for studies in his method of cheese-making. They watched his exact method and then returned home and did likewise. Most of them reported to him that the results were quite good but far below the standard of the cheese which he supplied. He could only reply to them that he believed that they must have left out the ingredients of love and religion which he put into his cheesemaking.

In the drying of my herbs I never use the quick method of sun-heat, or even worse, of fire-heat. They are dried painstakingly in shade by slow air-dehydration, with all the attendant worries of protecting them from pests such as moths and other destructive insects and field mice. But the results in fragrance and colour are worth the time given, this 'waiting upon the Lord' indeed. And the slowly-drying herbs scent my entire home—and even my life!

And despite all the difficulties of this modern life, the difficulties of children raised in the poisoned world concerning which Rachel Carson wrote so movingly and with such prophetic warning in her *Silent Spring*, I fully agree with my long-time friend Bette Butterworth that the present generation of children is a wonderful one. (And like Bette Butterworth, and countless other lovers of the world's youth, I do not accept their deaths in our modern wars, where warfare is now mass murder and no longer a question of personal valour.) In the Six-Day War in Israel I witnessed the terrible force of modern explosives; and shall never forget it. This letter comes to me from Bette as I come to the end of my book. I quote:

'I am MAD for all the young people here, they make the most beautiful songs which they come, with their "gitars", and sing to me. They have a great love of beauty and a great understanding. Some are already fighting in Vietnam and their letters are sad beyond belief. Wot to do? I wonder if you understand this?'

Yes, I understand.

We all accept now the bitter fact that even if we manage to raise healthy children, who in turn are willing to try and keep their bodies healthy by the eating of natural foods, sun and air-bathing, swimming and horse-riding (only never to be among the diet or athletic fanatics!), there are nuclear bombs in the possession of man, in many nations (and not all of them wise and moderate nations), which could in one explosion destroy millions of human lives and all of the far-stretching regions where such ill-fated humans may dwell.

And even now there come the Bomb air currents following experimental nuclear explosions, carrying atomic fall-out far and wide and doing unseen damage which no one has yet been able properly to examine or estimate.

Too early our children become aware of this horrible threat to their lives: they say little concerning this, but I am sure that in quiet moments they think much about this seemingly insoluble problem.

However, the History of the World clearly reveals that even in the darkest periods of the human race there was always a star of hope shining. And today we can take hope in the knowledge that this beautiful world was never made for man alone, he is only a sharer along with the birds and beasts, trees and plants, the fish in the sea and the tiny organisms in the mud. We learnt as children that before the destruction of the former world, careful provision was made for the animals: indeed God gathered far more animals than human beings into the safety of the Ark, and furthermore careful instructions were issued as to the provision of suitable foods so that the saved animals should not starve as they travelled to a new cleansed land. Therefore, it seems unlikely that man will be able at any time to destroy the world in which he has never yet become all-powerful. Unless he has a knife or a gun in his hands man will still flee from an attacking 'vegetarian' wild bear if he is able. Furthermore, while man has the new toy at his command, this tremendous toy enabling him to take flights to the moon, he is not likely to destroy the base from which he needs to fly.

For those who live close to Nature, each day dawns clean and beautiful, and we can share it with our family and the animals and birds, plants and trees, which are all around us. Close to Nature! The winds blow wild and the sun shines, the rains come and snow comes also, all wonderful things. We will refuse to let the folly of others mar our lives completely. Our neighbours may poison-spray their premises and land, and the stench temporarily drowns the scents of the opening lemon blossom and the sun-warmed herbs in our own garden. But the wind will come and cleanse the air once more; always the wind comes. And always

CONCLUSION

I am thinking of and agreeing with the words which the strange traveller and writer George Borrow took for the world from those Nature Children, the Gypsies:

'Life is very sweet, brother! there are the sun, moon, stars, all sweet things, and likewise the wind on the heath!'

[Note: When collecting wild foods and herbs, because we now live in an age of poison-sprayed countrysides, care must be taken to ensure that wild foods gathered have not been poisoned by spraying.]

AFTERWORD

The English edition of this book on the natural care of children was published in December 1970. Strangely, as if in support of this book, there soon appeared two dramatic reports concerning nature children. One was a newly discovered case, the other was a film made about a well-known historical 'wild child' who lived in a forest.

Both reports gave authentic evidence of human children who had survived in the wild without any assistance from other humans. They were young people who had grown up from infancy without any need of cooked or canned foods, vitamin pills, sheltered accommodation, and suchlike. They had grown up like Gypsy children, in kinship with nature and with wild animals; but, more remarkable than Gypsy children, they had known no human parental care since their early months. (One had supposedly fed from the udder of an animal, for he had taken the form of one—a gazelle—and moved on all fours.)

As most of the world now lives under the threat of atomic warfare and the consequent devastation that such warfare would bring, it is wise to know how to live without the need of food stores and drugstores, cooking stoves, and doctors, and to know how this can be done without any harm to personal health. Indeed, the health of the wild children was discovered to be superior to that of an average person raised in society.

The Jerusalem Post (December 1970) reported the case of a 'gazelle-boy'. First news of the discovery of this boy in the Spanish Sahara was in radio programmes. Then I looked for news in the daily papers and found the following:

'Gazelle-boy' Found in Sahara

A twenty-year-old human male who leaps like a gazelle and can run fifty kilometres an hour—on all fours—has been found living in the Spanish Sahara near Rio de Oro. The discovery of this feral child was reported to the Geneva Institute de la Vie by a French researcher, Jean-Claude Armen. He said the 'gazelle-boy' lives on roots and dates. Although he runs with his arms and legs, he is capable of standing erect.

Dr. Paul Rouget, director of the Institute, opinioned that the boy probably fell off a camel when a couple of months old and was adopted by gazelles. Dr. Rouget said that the boy will probably be able to survive until the age of about fifty, as long as he is not removed from his natural habitat.

The film in question is *L'Enfant Sauvage* (*The Wild Child*, as released in the United States), directed by François Truffaut. It is based on an extraordinary report published in France in 1806 by a Dr. Jean Itard. This true story of a wild boy is often mentioned in psychology books.

It tells of a country doctor who brought into his home (eight years before publication of his report) a twelve-year-old male animal and of his attempt to civilise him. To quote from a review in the *New Statesman* (January 1971):

The wild boy, found loose in the forests of Aveyron, had apparently been abandoned by his parents in infancy; one of several scars indicated that an attempt had been made to cut his throat; he was filthy, naked, a thing incapable of speech or reason. Itard rescued him from a deaf-and-dumb institution and possible incarceration in a lunatic asylum. Helped by his housekeeper, he set out to convert this curiosity, whom smart Parisians flocked for a while to see, into a rational human being. The word is that he never fully achieved his aim: Victor de L'Aveyron, as the boy came to be called, was to die in his thirties, still bereft of language. . . . there are the immaculate intimate details of the training: the wooden letters, the guided soup spoon, the intractable shoes, the games with walnut and cups, the small rewards of a glass of water or milk. . . . Throughout the boy yearns for his lost wilderness of the woods of Aveyron while Itard's pen scratches on, recording progress. . . .

AFTERWORD

At the time of writing this Afterword, hunters in Israel brought back a huge boar they had shot in our valley, beyond Tiberias. As the hunters were my neighbours, I saw the dead animal. They all agreed that the wild boar was a *muktar,* a sheikh, the leader of the wild pigs of the region. I marvelled at the size and beautiful conformation of this animal, and at the size and lustre of its wonderful teeth, with the side tusks like two daggers of ivory. I felt sad that the valley had been robbed of something so perfect and rare. I believed that the trees, the rocks, the paths and trails must miss the presence of that great creature who had grown up there.

I told the hunters that the death of that wild boar was a tragedy and that they should have spared a creature who was so special in every way. But the hunters defended their deed by describing the damage to local agriculture such an animal could cause. By their account of the boar's food needs, I learned of the vegetarian diet of the wild boar.

Of wild foods it would eat roots of many kinds, grasses, oats, mushrooms (in large quantities) and lichens, fruits, berries and nuts (especially the fruits of the wild arbutus and the *dom,* or Christ-thorn, trees, the acorns of the wild oaks, and carob pods). From cultivated fields it would take, in vast amounts, vegetables of all kinds, cereals (especially corn cobs and wheat), melons, bananas, grapes, citrus fruits, and avocados. And all of this eating involves much uprooting, trampling, and damage to crops.

Nonetheless, the diet described is an instinctive health diet indeed, and on this and an abundance of unhindered exercise, there had grown up a wild creature of a magnificence of build and health, that no domestic animal under man's dominance could ever achieve.

Rosh Pinna, Galilee
April 1971

INDEX

❧❧❧